Ghost
Dogs
of
the
South

John F. Blair, Publisher   Winston-Salem, North Carol

Ghost Dogs
of
the
South

by Randy Russell and Janet Barnett

Published by John F. Blair, Publisher

*The paper in this book meets the guidelines
for permanence and durability of the
Committee on Production Guidelines for
Book Longevity of the Council on Library Resources.*

Library of Congress Cataloging-in-Publication Data

Russell, Randy.
Ghost dogs of the South / by Randy Russell and Janet Barnett.
p.   cm.
ISBN 0-89587-229-3 (alk. paper)
I. Animal ghosts. 2. Dogs—Miscellanea. I. Barnett, Janet. II. Title.

BF1484.R87 2001
398.2'0975'05—dc21

2001035878

Design by Debra Long Hampton

This book is fondly dedicated
to the memory of

Desdemona

the sweetest, dumbest
Great Dane that ever lived.
The important things in life never really leave.

Contents

Foreword

When I asked students in my folklore classes to rapidly sketch the image of a ghost, the most frequent result from American students was a friendly, white-sheeted form with two round eyes and a ruffled hemline—definitely Casper-esque. Students from other countries drew interesting variants that reflected the ghost lore of their own cultures. But never in thirty years did anyone from any culture draw a phantom in the form of a dog. Does this mean that every dog has its day, after which it's relegated to oblivion? Not if the thousands of legends, beliefs, myths, customs, and personal-experience narratives from around the world are any indication.

Certainly, it is true that some cultures abhor dogs. For instance, in biblical literature, there are numerous negative references to dogs but only a single positive one—and that is found in the Book of Tobit, which was relegated to the Apocrypha. Tobit's dog served his blind master faithfully in a seeing-eye capacity, which was doubtless the redeeming factor that earned the lowly canine a neutral line or two in the text.

In general, however, most cultures view dogs as positive actors on the world stage. They herd domestic animals, pull sleds, guard property, hunt for game, offer companionship, lead the dead to the Other World, serve as food, entertain at the circus, sniff for contraband, rescue the perishing, and in some societies function as demigods that bring fortune to those who worship them. What other animal plays so many roles so well? It is no wonder that, at least in the Western world, the dog is regarded as man's best friend. This strong bond makes it easy for many to believe that dogs, like people, have spirits that sometimes return to earth after death.

Those who have personally witnessed a dog ghost need no convincing. Huston Smith, in his book *Why Religion Matters*, relates a first-person experience shared by John Neihardt, author of *Black Elk Speaks*. Neihardt and his wife had been involved in a minor car accident and were visited shortly thereafter by their insurance agent. All three were seated at the dining-room table while the agent took notes on the incident. Suddenly, he said, "I'm sorry, but your dog is making me nervous. Would you mind putting him out?" Startled, the Neihardts asked, "Dog? What dog are you talking about?" "Why, you know," replied the agent, "the little black Spaniel that's under the table." He bent to peer below the table, then shrugged. "Well, he's not there now. He slipped out, so never mind." The Neihardts exchanged glances but let the topic drop. What they didn't tell the agent was that only a week before, their beloved black Spaniel had died of old age.

While I was attending a "Folklore of the Supernatural" conference at Utah State a few years ago, a fellow conferee told me that her boyfriend—a confirmed skeptic about all things supernatural—had recently changed his mind. His parents had retired to the Southwest, and he was occupying the family home while attending classes at the local university. One day, he was called out of class by a frantic message that his house was on fire. He drove home at record speed, only to find the house a smoking ruin. Shocked, he climbed out of his car and identified himself to one of the firemen. "I'm really sorry," said the fireman. "We got here four minutes after the call came in, but the place was already an inferno. We just couldn't save it. Your dog did make it out, thank God." The student shrugged. "That's the least of my worries. I don't even have a dog." But the fireman insisted, "Well, I saw it! Big white-and-tan Collie. The front door was a ring of fire, but he came running right out through it. Beautiful dog. He was burned, but he was scared to death. I whistled at him and called, but he wouldn't stay." The student stared at the fireman in amazement. "Well," he stammered, "we used to have a big white-and-tan Collie, but he died five years ago—in the house."

These are two examples of dogs that became ghosts— "dog ghosts," in other words. Oral tradition is also full of humans who die and return as ghosts in the shape of dogs. These are "ghost dogs." Sometimes, it is a mother who returns to cover a sleeping baby or bring food to a hungry child. Sometimes, it is a friend or a family member who comes back to warn or to protect. But often, the ghost dog seems destined simply to terrorize.

Recently, my level-headed son and his wife spent a weekend in Charleston, South Carolina, and left to drive home to Atlanta late in the afternoon. Because they enjoy the countryside, they chose a picturesque two-lane road instead of the freeway. Twilight in the Low Country comes on fast; very soon, it was dark. With his wife drowsing at his side, my son switched on the headlights and slowed down to fifty-five miles an hour. He described what happened next. "Suddenly, the lonely stretch of road seemed eerie for no apparent reason, as if we had driven into a patch of evil. Up ahead, I saw what I first thought was a deer. It was about ten feet back from the pavement, standing at a forty-five-degree angle, staring at us as we came toward it. Its huge eyes were what startled me. At least four feet above the ground, they were a brilliant blue! As we drew closer, I could see that it wasn't a deer. It was an enormous dog, bigger than any dog could possibly be, a shaggy giant with matted gray hair. I got a glimpse of white teeth as we passed, and a horrible red tongue that hung out of its mouth. Its eyes were fixed on me with total malevolence. It's hard to explain, but I felt an irrational terror. I stepped on the gas and yelled, 'Honey, did you see that?' But she had been staring out in the opposite direction and had missed those frightful blue eyes completely. There was no way I would ever have turned around and gone back to investigate. In fact, I kept watching the rearview mirror for the next five miles, half expecting to see the . . . whatever it was . . . come loping after us."

There are plenty of folks in the Low Country who could have told him what he saw: a plat-eye. The concept of the plat-eye, derived from West Indian beliefs, is familiar to many African-Americans in Georgia and to speakers of Gullah in South Carolina. Oral tradition holds that a plat-eye is the evil ghost of a person who did not receive proper burial. He might have been shoveled into a too-shallow grave or tumbled under the sod in an awkward posture, buried without a priest or a prayer. Unable to find rest, the plat-eye is doomed to haunt the area in the form of a hideous dog with glowing eyes. Interestingly, neither my son nor his wife had ever heard of a plat-eye.

Another type of spectral dog figures prominently in the lore of the British Isles. Although different areas have their own special names for the creature, it is often referred to as simply "the Black Dog." Usually, it is vested with demonic qualities that strike terror in the heart of hapless souls who encounter it on moor or fen. But not all Black Dogs are evil. A student mesmerized my folklore class one day with the story of an afternoon she spent as a child on the tip of a peninsula jutting into the sea near Cape Town, South Africa. Her father had brought his wife and little girl from England so the family could be together while he was teaching at the university. One afternoon while her mother was ironing, the little girl stood idly looking out the window. She was surprised to see an enormous black dog walk slowly across the lawn and disappear around the corner of the house. Even more surprising, it came around the house again, padding silently along the same path. She had never seen it in the neighborhood before. When it made a third round, she called, "Mummy, Mummy! Come see this big black dog." Her mother came to the window, took one look, and gave a startled cry. Grabbing her daughter, she pulled her away from the window and wrapped her arms around her. "That's all right, darling," she gasped. "Don't be afraid. Mummy's right here. Everything's going to be all right. Daddy will be home soon." Her hysteria communicated itself to the little girl, who clung to her mother in terror without knowing why. Very soon, the professor came home. His wife ran to him and burst into tears. The little girl had never seen her mother cry, and that was far more frightening than the big dog. Then her mother revealed something she had never told them before. In her family back in England, there had been a secret tradition for many generations concerning the Black Dog. It appeared to some member of the family only when acute danger was present. Its role was to guard family members and protect them from harm. Though she had never seen the Black Dog herself, she recognized it the moment she looked out the window. Instantly, she knew that she and her little girl were in danger. Her husband listened calmly and soothed his wife and daughter. The rest of the evening passed tranquilly. But the next morning when they were having breakfast, the professor switched on the news. They listened, transfixed, to an announcement that the convicted murderer who had escaped from prison the day before had been recaptured. He told police he had spent the previous afternoon hiding in the bushes around a big house out on the tip of the peninsula.

Dennis Bardens, author of *Psychic Animals: A Fascinating Investigation of Paranormal Behavior,* relates an intriguing case from the Civil War era in which a dog ghost saved his master's life. A young man, sleeping with his dog in a haystack, was surprised by Union soldiers and taken prisoner. A search revealed documents that proved he was a spy for the Confederate army. The colonel in charge wasted no time in sentencing him to be hanged early the next morning. The young spy asked if his dog could be allowed to sleep with him that night, but the colonel curtly refused. As soon as the prisoner was led away, the officer gave orders to have the dog killed immediately. It was clubbed to death with rifle butts. Early in the morning, the prisoner was taken to the place of execution. He asked the riflemen if his dog had been given something to eat. Embarrassed to reveal the truth, they assured the doomed man that they had taken good care of it. At that moment, the spy looked down at the ground a few feet in front of him and broke into a grin. "Ah, there you are, old boy," he said, staring at seemingly empty space. "I knew my best buddy would come to say goodbye!" The members of the firing squad exchanged glances and hastily blindfolded the man. They took their positions and waited for the officer to give the order to fire. When they heard nothing, they looked at the colonel and saw that his gaze was riveted on the bare earth in front of the prisoner. His face had turned a sickly white. After a prolonged pause, he seemed to shake himself out of a daze. "Execution deferred!" he cried, and hurried from the scene. That night, the Confederates attacked, and the colonel was killed in the resulting skirmish. The spy was freed by his own army units. For the rest of his life, he delighted in telling how the ghost of his dog had come back to save him from the firing squad.

One of the special skills often attributed to man's best friend is that dogs can see ghosts that may or may not be visible to their masters. A respected citizen of Athens, Georgia, came to my class to relate his experience with the ghost of a Gypsy girl who haunted his home on Boulevard Avenue. "I didn't believe in such things as ghosts," he told us, "until the evening I glanced up from my book and saw this young woman standing in the corner of the room. My little dog jumped right up and froze in position, staring straight at her. Then she just faded away. I was really glad that little dog saw her, too, or I'd have thought for sure I was losing my mind."

English novelist Elizabeth Goudge, writing her life's reminiscences in *The Joy of the Snow*, shares many personal encounters with the inexplicable. At one time, she and her friend Jessie purchased a three-hundred-year-old Oxfordshire cottage, inhabited before her death by a spunky old lady who had been the village washerwoman. The new owners soon became aware of her presence. One evening while Jessie was at a meeting and Elizabeth was writing at one end of the living room, their dog, Tike, suddenly sprang to its feet and began to bark furiously at an invisible something near the fireplace. This eerie scenario was replayed on other lonely evenings until finally the author abandoned the living room and took to writing upstairs with Tike ensconced on her bed. Evidently, the ghost felt free to accompany them. As Goudge describes it, Tike "did not bark but she would sit up, lift her head high and growl at someone who apparently came into the room, and then her head would move round slowly as her dark eyes watched that someone wander round the room and go out again."

A fascinating incident occurred several years ago at the site of a restored plantation home in Georgia. A young attorney who was interested in historic preservation volunteered to live in a mobile home on the property and serve as night caretaker. One night, he and a friend from Atlanta took their dinner dates home very late. He invited his friend to be his guest for the night and save the long drive back to the city for the morning. Around two o'clock in the morning, he was awakened by the furious barking of his dogs. Sensing that something was very wrong, he shook his friend awake and armed himself with a rifle. The two men stole silently out into the night, guided by the sounds of the dogs. There was a wispy ground fog, but a pale, high-riding moon lessened the darkness. In a few moments, they could make out the dogs, clustered at a corner of the old mansion and barking frantically at something hidden from view behind the house. Cautiously, the two men approached the corner and peered around. To their utter amazement, they were face to face with four men on horseback. All four wore faded uniforms of the Confederate army, and they sat their horses with an air of infinite weariness. The men and the soldiers stared silently at each other. Nobody moved; nobody said a word. Even the dogs were hushed. After a long moment, the lead soldier slowly turned his horse, and the four figures moved silently away through the tattered fog. The dogs resumed their frenzied barking but made no move to follow the phantom figures. Neither did the two men.

So there we have it: dog ghosts, ghost dogs, and live dogs that see ghosts; dogs that are afraid of ghosts and dogs that are fearless (as an old Appalachian jingle affirms, "Over the hill and 'cross the level,/Grandpap's Bulldog treed the devil").

You don't have to believe in ghosts to enjoy this book, but you should believe in dogs. Just days before he died, Mark Twain wrote a humorous piece advising folks as to strategies for getting through the Pearly Gates. His final recommendation was this: "Leave your dog outside. Heaven goes by favor. If it went by merit, you would stay out and the dog would go in."

Randy Russell and Janet Barnett are the right authors to have written *Ghost Dogs of the South*. They not only empathize with dogs, they have the knack of speaking from the standpoint of a dog—of making a dog, even a ghostly one, as multidimensional as your next-door neighbor. In this collection, they have given us an exceptionally rich offering of tales that illuminate the shadow side of man's best friend.

Genelle Morain, Ph.D.
Professor Emeritae, University of Georgia

Preface

As folklorists who specialize in researching and collecting ghost stories, we routinely ask the people we know if they have ever encountered a ghost. When novelist Nancy Pickard told us her only ghost experience was a nocturnal visit from her deceased American Eskie, Sasha, we realized that our own most poignant ghost encounter was the lingering visitation of our companion Desdemona. A black Great Dane with unclipped ears, Desdemona continued to guard the landing at the top of our stairs for weeks beyond her death. When someone came to the door, her ghost clambered down the wooden staircase to greet the visitor. The sound of a Great Dane rushing down oak steps is not easily mistaken or easily ignored. We heard it. Desdemona was there. The most difficult part of this experience was when we came home and, while fiddling with the front-door key, listened to the ghost of our dog coming downstairs to greet us, knowing that when we opened the door, she wouldn't be there.

Nancy's visit from Sasha was a quieter experience. Nancy felt the weight of her former pet settle on the mattress when she went to bed. Sasha was there.

"I didn't see her, you understand, but I felt her," Nancy explained. "Soon after she died, I went with friends to Casa Dega, a little town in Florida where only psychics live and where they do readings in their homes. In a reading in which my psychic didn't seem to get anything else right, she suddenly said, 'There's a little white dog here who wants to say hello to you. She wants you to know she's fine.'

"I really needed that message, too, because I felt so bad about her death."

Nancy's experience with Sasha started us on our journey to uncover as many stories of dogs, in both the recorded and living catalog of Southern folklore, as time and energy might allow. We were not disappointed. The dog is part of the soil of the American South.

It would take a hundred years to begin to understand dogs' love of human companionship. They'll put up with anything just to be with us. We do not attempt to explain it. In putting together the small collection of stories for this volume, we did, however, concentrate on stories that illustrate the relationship between dogs and people.

Speaking of illustrations, the antique photographs accompanying these stories are from the authors' personal collection. The photos date from the 1890s to about 1915. Most were produced as postcards. It was popular in this period of American history to have one's home photos printed with postcard backs. Many included here are amateur photos. Others were made at the local photographer's studio. Most, if not all, are unique images.

The photographs are meant to illustrate this book in a general way and to remind us that the companionship of a beloved dog is not a passing fancy. It was our goal to select photos that captured a moment of the relationship between people and their dogs, or vice versa. Each of the photos is one of our favorites. The placement of the photos in the book is not intended to directly illustrate the accompanying stories. We hope these photos enhance the reader's experience a small portion of the degree to which dogs have enriched our lives.

Sources for researching folklore are varied. Primary sources are those collected from an oral telling. They may be found in previously published collections, journals, letters, diaries, songs, and research papers turned in at school. Libraries throughout the South house excellent collections of old newspaper clippings, a most valuable source of local folklore.

A story heard is a story told. The real American folklore, we believe, exists in the telling. Storytellers preserve the folklore of a community. We are indebted to, and our research has been enriched by, living repositories of local stories.

Carrie Gates holds many of her family's stories from the Little Canada community in a remote section of the mountains of western North Carolina. We'd like to thank Carrie for granting us permission to share the story of a Civil War haunting her grandmother told. It is the basis for the retelling we have titled "Devil Dog."

Artisan and Native American storyteller Freeman Owl patiently taught us how to see Cherokee towns and villages in western North Carolina that are no longer there. A stone carver of unsurpassed artistry, he keeps the history of an entire nation in his heart.

Many others helped us in our research and writing of the stories in this collection.

Lia Matera aided in our understanding of "Belly Dog." Similarly, Judith Kelman offered needed advice as we readied "Jameson's Bell" for publication.

For the past few years, we have been presenters at an annual, week-long "True Ghosts" seminar sponsored by the North Carolina Center for the Advancement of Teaching, located in Cullowhee. NCCAT provides North Carolina public-school teachers with enrichment seminars throughout the calendar year and has served as a model for other states in providing similar opportunities for the dedicated professionals who teach school. It is our great pleasure to be associated in even a small way with this ongoing effort. Carrie Gates, mentioned above, is an NCCAT associate who works tirelessly to provide the services necessary for many successful enrichment seminars at the Cullowhee facility. We'd like to thank her and Henry Wong, an NCCAT fellow, for including us in one of the many seminars they prepare each year. Henry also continues to enhance our appreciation of

North Carolina folkways through his performance of guitar, mandolin, and voice. Much of the original folklore of the South is contained in the songs of generations past.

We simply would be unable to touch the richness of Southern folklife without being able to enjoy the performance of traditional music. Ballads sung from childhood memory by Mary Jane Queen of rural western North Carolina help keep us in touch with the soul of the South. Henry Queen, her son, has always proved generous with us of his endless talents on banjo and guitar. A remarkable husband-and-wife team, Gaye and Phil Johnson of Tryon, North Carolina, share their incredible talents with audiences throughout the South. Gaye Johnson is the purest alto voice ever to bring traditional lyrics to life. When she sings, you are lifted from the ground. Phil Johnson, a master on both acoustic and resonator guitar, is also a noted songwriter and a marvelous storyteller. Together, they capture more of life than any book can hold. We'd like to thank the two of them for keeping us in touch with what matters of culture. Both can be heard by visiting their home on the internet at www.radioyur.com.

This book would not have been possible without the enthusiastic support of the entire staff of John F. Blair, Publisher, in Winston-Salem, North Carolina. To the authors' delight, Steve Kirk, whose own work has appeared in *The Best American Short Stories* series, edited the original manuscript we turned in. Artist Debra Long Hampton designed this book and painstakingly prepared and adjusted each of the antique photographs for the printed page. She also created the cover, one we believe deserves a frame. Carolyn Sakowski, Anne Waters, Ed Southern, and Ken Rumble were each instrumental in guiding our original proposal toward publication, and each continues to work hard to see that this book finds its way into the hands of readers. Without marketing, sales, promotion, and publicity, most books would sit stacked in sealed cartons in the warehouse. Like dogs, books need to breathe, and we thank the staff of John F. Blair for giving ours a brisk walk in sunshine and air.

We are pleased to acknowledge the friendship of Genelle Morain, who kindly found time in her busy schedule to write the foreword to this book. Dr. Morain's intellectual accomplishments pale only in comparison to her personal charm. Her teaching of comparative folklore fills a gap in the body of folk study—the one of grace.

Finally, we'd like to thank all those dogs everywhere who so eagerly do everything they can to get along with us. We don't deserve it.

Randy Russell
Janet Barnett

Ghost
Dogs
of
the
South

Watch Dog

Harlan County, Kentucky

At the end of World War II, Corbin Forrest went to work in the Star Company coal mine in southeastern Kentucky. He and his wife lived in company housing, and he walked to work each morning with his dog, an Airedale he named Mike in honor of a friend who had been killed in France during the big push that followed D-Day.

Mike could tell time. Because of this, and as something

of a joke, Corbin hung his pocket watch on Mike's collar when he went to work and left the dog outside the mine entrance. He'd ask the other miners during his shift if they had seen his watch dog when they'd come into work that day. Corbin often bragged to the other workers in the No. 7 mine that he didn't need a watch anyway. It had been his father's pocket piece, or he would have sold it years ago.

Mike sat outside the mine but inside the company fence. He was tolerated by the foreman. He wasn't a particularly friendly dog to strangers, but he didn't really bother anyone. Besides, Mike was good for a dollar bet when there was an employee new to the No. 7.

Miners worked six days a week back then. And six days a week at 12:14, Mike would spring to his feet and run inside the No. 7. In a minute, he'd find Corbin and his crew breaking for lunch. He was always there when Corbin opened his pail. Mike waited patiently until his master was through eating. Then he was given half of Corbin's second sandwich as a reward. Corbin packed his lunchpail and handed it to Mike. The Airedale carried it by the handle through the mine tunnels and back outside. There, he guarded it jealously until the shift ended. When Corbin emerged from the tunnel at shift's end, he unclipped his watch from Mike's collar, and the two of them walked home.

Two of the miners put up a makeshift shelter, just a few boards and a piece of corrugated tin, for Mike to wait under when it rained. Someone painted the dog's name on the tin, and Mike became the official mascot of Star Company's No. 7 mine.

Corbin could be a talkative fellow. He was tall and gangly and had an easy grin. Of course, once a miner's been at it for an hour or two, he can look like he has the biggest smile known to man. That's because his face is covered in black dust. When he smiles, the only thing you see are lots of teeth and the pink and red of his gums. A miner's smile shines like a flashbulb going off.

Unlike some of the other veterans in the mines, Corbin didn't have much to say about his experiences in the war. It was the one thing he'd found in life that was worse than working in a coal mine. He'd seen Dover. He'd seen France. And that was all he had to say about World War II.

The air-shaft watchman, at his post outside, saw Mike get up from his resting place and run to the mine entrance too early for lunch one day. It was long before anyone heard the rumbling.

"Must have set his watch wrong," the fan operator said to himself.

Inside the No. 7, at the end of a spur where Corbin was working, the crew stopped when they heard Mike's barking. It echoed through the mine. The Airedale was standing right behind them.

"Hey, Corbin, I think your watch broke. It's not 12:14 yet."

"What's up, boy?" Corbin asked the dog.

Mike stopped barking, rushed to his master, and whined. He reached for Corbin's hand. Corbin tried to pet him, but Mike put his mouth on his master's hand and pulled insistently, still whining. Corbin knew what Mike was doing. He knew it instantly.

"Get out!" he yelled to the crew. "Drop your tools and run!"

Miners don't kid around like that. Work in a coal mine is too dangerous for teasing miners' fears. There was no mistaking the urgency in Corbin's voice. Not a single crew member hesitated to do as he was told. Hollering to other workers along the way, the men ran out of the spur and up the long, ascending tunnel to the No. 7 entrance. The train-car operator soon joined them outside.

Forty-six miners stood in a group outside the mine entrance. Some had grabbed their lunchpails.

"What are we doing out here?" one of them asked.

"Corbin said to get the heck out, and we did."

Corbin didn't know how to explain it. Mike knew what was what. That was all he would have said, if he had said anything.

"The company will dock us all if we stand around out here much longer," the foreman said.

"Better wait a minute," Corbin said.

Corbin Forrest had made Mike's acquaintance on active duty in France. They were on the push after D-Day, backing the Germans to Paris and, they hoped, beyond. The

Nazis were in retreat when Corbin was sent to an advance emergency landing ground for two United States air squadrons. The area was hot, receiving shells from the retreating German forces, who hoped to destroy the landing strip on their way out.

Corbin and one of his buddies, Robert Wright of New York City, pulled duty in the cookhouse, a quickly erected shanty open on one end, where meals were to be prepared for the air-support crews. Mike showed up, a rangy, skinny-looking, wire-haired dog. His legs were too long for his body, Corbin thought. The Airedale's dense fur was brown with black markings. Mike's nose was long, and his fur extended from the sides of his snout and from under his chin, giving him the distinct appearance of wearing a mustache and a goatee. His ears were small and V-shaped. They folded to the side. Mike looked somewhat elegant for a dog. He also looked hungry.

Corbin and Robert Wright fed the starving Airedale, and a fast friendship was instantly formed between men and dog.

"You think he speaks German or French?" Robert asked.

There was no way to know.

The cookhouse was one of only two structures at the landing area. The other was the latrine. A few tents had been pitched, but they generally held supplies. The soldiers, who had seen plenty of heavy fire, preferred to eat and sleep in foxholes and trenches dug for the purpose.

They were there two days when the first plane landed at the emergency strip. It had been damaged by German flak and was losing fuel. When it touched the weedy runway, it tumbled forward and burst into flames. The American soldiers were in a grim mood. Their only relief was petting the dog when they came to the cookhouse for heated rations.

Interested in a few moments' diversion, different soldiers tried different ways to lure Mike from his cookhouse post, hoping to engage the dog in a bit of play. One bounced a ball, tossed it, and yelled "Fetch!"

Mike sat down where he was.

"The dog don't speak English," Robert Wright said.

Another rubbed canned meat on a rag and tied it to a stick. Mike licked the rag when it was held under his nose but wouldn't budge an inch when the soldier took it away. The Airedale knew where the food was kept.

"Maybe if you had a French Poodle in a tutu, he'd go for that," Robert told the soldier.

Corbin laughed. He hadn't laughed in days.

After the plane came in, and even though it went up in flames, the Germans became more interested in destroying the landing area before they were forced by the oncoming American troops to abandon the region altogether. A long-range gun was set up two miles away, and shells came in at regular intervals, leaving a random pattern of smoking holes in the ground. The Germans seemed to be aiming at nothing in particular.

A couple shells came in close to the cookhouse at about eleven o'clock one morning. Corbin checked his watch.

"Just in case it happens," he told Robert, "I want to know what time it is when I die."

"They say you don't hear the one that gets you," Robert told him.

Maybe *people* don't.

Just then, Mike became restless. He walked around the large iron boilers in the cookhouse, then paced in and out. Finally, he sat down outside and howled. Like a wolf, he howled. Corbin didn't know an Airedale could do that.

"Must be he don't like what we're cooking," Robert said. "What did you put in the stew this time, Corbin?"

Mike stopped howling. He leapt to his feet and came quickly into the cookhouse and began threading himself between Robert's feet, walking between his legs.

"Get away, will you?"

The Airedale barked furiously at this rebuke. Corbin bent down to pet him, hoping it would calm the dog. As soon as Corbin put out his hand, Mike took it in his mouth and tugged at it, his teeth not quite breaking the skin. It was clear the dog wanted Corbin to come outside with him.

"Come on, Robert," Corbin said. "He's got something to show us, and he isn't going to wait."

"Maybe he's got a family of puppies in the woods he wants us to feed," Robert said. "What the heck, can't hurt this stew any if we burn it."

Mike let go of Corbin's hand, and they followed the dog. The Airedale was at full trot. He led the two soldiers to a shell hole about thirty yards from the cookhouse. In they went, the three of them. The soldiers sat down to keep out of the wind. Robert lit a cigarette. He handed it to Corbin, who took a drag and handed it back.

It was a nice-enough shell hole, but Robert had seen shell holes before. When the cigarette was out, he thought he would go. But Mike wouldn't let him.

When the soldier stood up, the dog became suddenly ferocious. The Airedale drew back his lips to show his teeth and growled. His eyes were on fire, it seemed to Robert. The soldier sat back down.

Mike stared up at the sky, then glanced at Corbin, shifting his eyebrows, then looked to the sky once more. He heard the whine of the artillery shell before the men did. The shrill incoming whine was immediately followed by a crashing sound and a loud blast. Dirt and small bits of debris rained down on the shell hole in which the men cowered in the company of the Airedale.

The shell had hit the cookhouse dead on. Corbin and Robert stared at each other in near disbelief. But they believed, all right. They sure did.

Mike showed no further interest in them. Scrabbling from the shell hole, the dog rushed to the wreckage of the cookhouse, where he greedily foraged all the food he could find. It was an outdoor barbecue, as far as Mike was concerned, and he was the only one invited.

"You know what I think?" Robert asked. "I think that dog snuck across the German lines and gave them the coordinates for the cookhouse, then came back here to wait for the feast."

Corbin thought differently. He thought he would do whatever it took to keep Mike. He managed, through bribery and begging, to have the dog transported to England, where Mike was quarantined. From there, the Airedale was shipped to Kentucky and eagerly adopted by Corbin's wife. She said it was the best letter home she'd ever received. The dog waited with her for the war to end and spent his time learning to understand American English.

<hr />

"Nothing's happening today," the foreman of the No. 7 announced, turning away from the group of coal diggers. He walked back to the mine entrance.

That's when Mike attacked him. Corbin had never seen his dog knock down a man before, but that's what Mike did. The Airedale sprang after the foreman, got within a yard of him, and leapt as high as he could, landing fifty pounds of dog in the middle of the foreman's back. The foreman fell to the ground with Mike on top of him.

Once he regained his wind, the foreman tried to get up, ready no doubt to fire someone on the spot. Mike showed his teeth and growled fiercely. Some of the men laughed. Corbin's pocket watch dangled unscathed from the dog's collar. It ticked away the seconds.

That's when they heard the rumbling underground. There was a slate fall at the end of the spur Corbin's crew had been drilling. The roof fell. A cloud of black dust belched from the entrance to the No. 7. A funnel of dust rose from the air shaft.

The men stood silent, pondering their near misfortune, waiting to see if there would be a fire. There was none. Mike returned to Corbin's side and accepted a scratch on his head. Soon, it would be time for lunch.

The foreman got to his feet, knocked the dirt from his shirt with both hands, then strode boldly toward Corbin and Mike. He reached his hand to his back pants pocket as he walked. No one was sure what would happen next. The foreman fumbled a dollar bill from a worn wallet and held the bill out to Corbin.

"Buy that damn dog some hamburger on your way home tonight," he said.

The miners laughed. Their bigger-than-life smiles cleared the air.

"I'll do that," Corbin promised, accepting the money.

One of the miners who had grabbed his lunchpail from habit as he exited the mine walked to Mike's makeshift shelter with its roof of corrugated tin. He opened his metal pail, took out a sandwich, and hurriedly unwrapped it. He set the food down at the shelter. Mike was over there in a flash to have at it.

Other miners who'd carried their pails followed suit. Those who hadn't done so returned to the mine when the all-clear was given and brought out portions of their lunch for Mike. The Airedale's stomach was so swollen he could barely manage the walk home with Corbin that evening.

The spur Corbin had been working became a central tunnel of the No. 7 over the years. Miners working the spur long after Corbin retired told new employees the reason there was an empty doghouse with a corrugated tin roof outside the Star Company mine. One of the miners—no one knew which one—repainted Mike's name on the tin in fresh white paint after the letters had flaked and weathered over time.

Star Company's No. 7 proved such a successful mine that it operated around the clock in the ensuing years. After Corbin and Mike were both dead, the company continued to pull coal from that hole. Miners working the night shift kept an ear out for what became known as "the ghost clock of the No. 7." Of course, some people say all coal miners work the night shift, because it is always night underground.

A miner's shift is full of strange and sometimes frightening sounds. Knocks and creaks, groans and wails echo through the mine. Above a miner's head, there is sometimes a constant crackling sound as the topping settles after a day of blasting. It sounds like the roof is falling in.

Somewhere, a rock or a large chunk of coal loosens from

a rib by its own force and drops with a tremendous thud heard throughout the mine. Deadly gases sometimes seep through crevices in the coal, creating an eerie, deadly hiss that is followed by a sound like the murmur of running water as more gas escapes.

The underground railway tracks contract and expand with changes in temperature and create a series of terrifying screeches, sudden pops, and prolonged groans. Water dripping in an isolated corner of a mine is magnified underground and can sound like the blows of a sledgehammer on solid stone.

It's no surprise that miners can be a little jumpy, even at sounds they can identify. Yet there is another, very different sound in the No. 7 mine. The sound is the ticking of a pocket watch. It moves through the mine as if carried by a ghost low to the ground.

When the ticking is heard, all work and conversation end. Where the ticking stops, an accident will occur. Unfailingly, the miners move away from the spot. Unfailingly, slate falls from the roof, or a fissure of rock fourteen times the size of a man slaps forward from a side wall and smashes to the mine floor. A coal car slips off its brakes, races backwards down the inclined railway tracks, and crashes into a wall of coal where moments before a miner was drilling.

After an accident, miners in the vicinity, miners who may have been hurt or killed if not for the warning, do not eat their lunch. Or if the accident occurs after lunch, they do not eat a noon meal the next shift. Instead, they unwrap their food and leave it in the makeshift doghouse outside the No. 7. They mean to keep that watch running. They have not forgotten Mike. And he has not forgotten them.

A Dog's Wish

Tryon, North Carolina

One Sunday after dark, in the early 1930s, Fayette and Bill Johnson walked the red-clay Wilderness Road with their dog, Lanier. Lanier was half Black Labrador Retriever and half something bigger. She carried a rubber ball in her mouth.

Bill carried a guitar. Fayette carried a pound of red clay sticking to the bottom of her shoes, and a song in her heart. They'd been to evening church. Fayette went to church to hear her grandmother sing. Bill went to church to play guitar. Fayette's granny had been dead for years, but when Fayette sat in church and the singing started, she could hear her grandmother clear as a bell.

Her granny sang loud and sang pretty. Although she wasn't there, her voice was. It stood out from the others, sweet like sugar.

"By and by we'll go to see them,/By and by we'll go to seem them,/By and by we'll go to see them on the other bright shore."

Lanier never came to church until after Fayette and Bill were already there. She would look around their yard on Aster Lane, that ball in her mouth, and notice after careful study that they weren't home anymore. Then she'd trot on over to the church on Wilderness Road and sit outside, the rubber ball in her mouth. She'd wait till the singing was over.

When the people came outside, Lanier would throw the ball to one of them. She'd lower her head and, with the ball at the tip of her mouth, jerk her head up and open her mouth at the same time. She could throw it straight, too. That ball would land right in front of you, unless it hit something and rolled to the side.

The idea was that you were supposed to pick up the ball and give it a toss in any direction. Lanier would get that ball, no matter how hard you threw it, before it stopped rolling. Sometimes, she would catch it on the first bounce. Then she would come running right at you, stop ten yards short, lower her head, and throw the ball at your feet. She'd loop it up high in the air.

The people at church knew from experience not to pick up the rubber ball and throw it. Lanier simply did not know the word *quit*. Once you threw the ball, she would get it just fine and throw it back to you. And back to you. And back to you. Over and over again. If you didn't pick up the ball after an entire minute went by, she'd come get it, walk away ten yards, turn around, and throw it right to your feet again. And again. And again.

The only way to keep from throwing that ball all day and all night was to not pick it up in the first place. Lanier would toss it to someone else then, looking for a person smart enough to learn the game of fetch.

This Sunday, the singing had been better than most. Everyone had kept at it until Bill thought his fingers were going to come off and get stuck in the strings of his guitar.

Darkness covered Wilderness Road before they were halfway home. That's when they met Colonel Ambrose Mills, coming the other way on the road at the edge of the Blue Ridge foothills.

Ambrose didn't know where his head was.

During the Revolutionary War, Ambrose Mills had been a colonel on the British side. Well, the British lost that war, and one of the places they lost it was at Kings Mountain. Ambrose escaped from that battle but was caught not far from Tryon, where the colonel had his house. When the other side wins a war, you lose things like your head and your house. Colonel Ambrose Mills lost both.

Fayette and Bill Johnson didn't know any of this when they met Ambrose walking along Wilderness Road that Sunday evening. They didn't recognize him anyway, because Ambrose Mills didn't have a head. He had on fine leather boots, britches, shirt and collar, coat and vest, but just raw neck where his head should be.

Lanier tossed her ball to Ambrose. It rolled right to his feet. When Fayette and Bill looked up and saw the man without a head standing in front of them on the road, the first thing they did was turn pale. The next thing they did was shake all over.

It isn't easy being a headless ghost. It takes years and years to learn to talk with your neck. And it takes even longer than that to learn to listen. Ambrose had been working on it for about 150 years. The worst part of it is, when you're a headless ghost and have spent all that time learning to converse, there aren't many people who will stick around long enough to talk with you.

"Hold it right there, if you please," Ambrose said.

Lanier ran forward, picked up her ball, trotted off ten yards, and threw it to the ghost again. She didn't care whether he had a head or not. He had an arm and a hand. She could train him, unless he was too stupid to learn.

Fayette and Phil wanted to turn tail and run. But they were too scared to move.

"I have a small favor to ask of you," Ambrose told them. "Please listen, and if you choose to assist me with the task,

I'll reward you. I have three barrels of gold and silver coins buried in the ground over to my place. There are many things, if you'll give it thought, that a ghost might be able to do for you. If you have a mortgage on your home, I could go into the bank and tear that paper up. Or I could file papers at the courthouse that say you own the entire county and always have."

"We're church-going people," Fayette said, finding her voice. "What you just offered would be cheating, and we'll have no part of that."

"Wait a second, honey," Bill said.

But Fayette kept right on talking fast.

"If you are the devil, I call on the Lord here on this road. Now, be off!"

Ambrose didn't go anywhere. Lanier retrieved her ball, trotted back, and tossed it to the ghost.

"I'm not the devil," Ambrose assured them. "Is there any way to make your dog stop doing that?"

"Not really," Bill said.

"Do you mind if I have a word with her?" Ambrose asked.

"Be my guest," Bill told him.

Ghosts can talk to dogs. Almost any ghost can. Ambrose told Lanier to stop throwing the ball.

Well, she'd heard that before. After a minute, she retrieved the ball from Ambrose's feet and trotted off ten yards, where she turned and threw the ball right back to him. Happiness for a Black Labrador Retriever is doing the same thing over again.

Ambrose picked up the rubber ball and put it in his coat pocket. Lanier sat down on her haunches, her tongue dangling, and stared at that pocket the whole while Ambrose talked. It was her ball, and she didn't intend to let him leave with it.

"If you're the devil, I call on God's lightning to come down from the sky and strike you into flames!" Fayette said.

Ambrose stood in front of her unignited.

"Hold on, honey," Bill said.

"If you're the devil, I pray the Lord to send bears from these very woods as we speak, to rip your body to bacon strips with their ferocious claws!"

"Hold on, now," Bill said to his wife. "He's not the devil. He's a ghost."

"My name is Colonel Ambrose Mills," the headless ghost told them.

And he told them the story of his death. He told them he'd been a wealthy man and said that rich men don't always know which side of a war to get in on. He apologized for choosing poorly.

"I was caught with eight other men on the British side. They hanged us on the spot. The Continental Army harbored no fondness for Loyalists to the British cause. The eight I was hanged alongside of were Captain Chitworth, Captain Grimes, Captain Walter Gilkey, Captain Wilson, Lieutenant Lafferty, John McFall, John Bebby, and Augustine Hobbs.

"Martha, who came to cut us loose, was the wife of Aaron Bickerstaff, who was killed at the Battle of Kings

Mountain. Friends of Captain Chitworth took his body on a plank to a graveyard at Bickerstaff's farm for burial. The rest of us, or I should say most of the rest of us, were buried very near where we're standing tonight in a trench no more than two feet deep.

"Your fine dog here could probably find the location without much trouble. But here's the trouble. That old man Martha brought with her to cut us down wasn't very good with a knife. I was the first one he worked on, and the rope was buried in the skin around my neck. They didn't use the right kind of knot. But that's to be understood. The men were in a hurry.

"When the old man tried to cut me down, he cut my head off instead. It sat there on the grass while he went to work on the others. By the time they had the trench dug, I somehow got buried without it."

"Why, that's just awful," Fayette said.

"It is that. You see, I can't rest until I get my head back. I was wondering if you two might help. Here, I have a likeness."

Ambrose reached into his pocket. Lanier came to all fours.

Ambrose removed a small oval of ivory, upon which his portrait had been painted in miniature. He handed it to Fayette.

"You can't see much at night, I know," Ambrose said. "But that's the head I'm looking for. Why don't you take that with you and study it in the morning? Then we can start the search."

He disappeared into the mist. The rubber ball fell to the road. Lanier had it in her mouth on the first bounce.

"Why can't he find his own head?" Fayette asked her husband once they were home.

"I don't know, darling. But you always hear tell of headless ghosts. It must be something they're not good at, not having any eyes and all."

Fayette and Bill Johnson were good Samaritans. They spent seven days looking for Ambrose's head. They came up empty.

Lanier, put off that no one had time to play toss-and-catch, spent his days clearing the family's pond of sticks. Tulip poplars grew along one side of the water, and there were always sticks, it seemed, floating on the pond. Lanier made a collection of them. She'd swim into the water like it was her steady job, retrieve a stick, then climb out of the pond with it, where she'd shake herself free of excess water. She'd carry the stick to a pile of pond sticks and add it to the mound. The first thing Lanier would do in the morning was check on her sticks. If any were missing, she wanted to know about it.

That Sunday just after dark, Colonel Ambrose Mills greeted Fayette and Bill Johnson as they walked home from church along Wilderness Road. Bill carried his guitar. Fayette carried a fresh pound of red clay stuck to the bottom of her shoes.

Lanier ran toward Ambrose and stopped ten yards short, where she ducked her head and raised it, throwing the rubber ball to the headless ghost. It rolled to a stop at Ambrose's feet. The ghost picked up the ball and put it in his coat pocket.

Ambrose knew they hadn't found his head. He thanked them for looking. He had one last thought.

"Do you have my portrait with you?"

Fayette said that she did.

"Would you mind if I show it to your dog? I think my head might be underwater."

"Only the devil can talk to dogs," Fayette said.

She took the ivory oval with Ambrose's face painted on it from her purse and handed it to the ghost.

"Oh, no, that's not so," Bill said. "All ghosts can talk to dogs. And dogs can talk back. Isn't that right, colonel?"

The headless ghost nodded that it was, but they couldn't see that.

"I have been dead a long time," Ambrose said, "and I haven't had a minute's rest. I cannot rest without my head. Now, it has taken me an incredibly long time to learn to speak, not having a mouth. And it's taken me a very long time to learn to hear, not having ears. But that's not the worst of it.

"Every time I approach someone, they scream and run away. I can't get out a decent 'How do you do?' before someone else starts throwing rocks at me. You're the first people I've met who've let me talk. I am very grateful for that."

"You're welcome," Bill told the ghost.

"This may be my only chance, you see, for another hundred years, and I am very tired. I would like to catch up on my sleep."

"All right, then," Fayette capitulated. "You can talk to the dog if you want."

"Just please don't leave with that ball in your pocket, or Lanier will pace the stairs all night and we won't get any sleep," Bill said.

Ambrose squatted down in the road on his boot heels. Lanier rushed over to say hello and to see if she could get her nose inside his coat pocket.

"This is the head I'm looking for," Ambrose said in dog talk. He showed Lanier the painting. "I have been dead longer than most of the ghosts you'll dig up around here. I have considerable influence on this side of living. Whatever it is you want, I'll try and get it done for you, if you can find my head."

Dogs can see in the dark better than people can, and Lanier was no exception. She threw her rubber ball to Bill, where it rolled to within inches of his feet, then darted off the road and down the slope among the bushes. She came quickly to a running creek. The water wasn't deep enough for her to swim in, so she pranced around in it until she found the spot with her nose.

Lanier dug the creek bottom and came up with a human skull. She carried it to the bank and went back for the jawbone. It still had its teeth. Lanier shook the water off and darted to a low place closer to the road. She dug there for a little bit until she came to bones. They weren't very deep at all.

Bill bounced the rubber ball in the road when he and Fayette grew tired of waiting.

Lanier came bounding back.

The next morning, they followed Lanier back to where she'd been digging. She took them to Ambrose's head, then led them to the place where the bones were buried.

Fayette and Bill walked to the preacher's house and told him their dog had found some bones to the side of Wilderness Road. All agreed that a proper interment was called for. Neighbors found a peaceful place under the pines. Nine graves were dug.

The bones of nine American Tories were buried, along with their silver coat buttons and belt buckles. The buttons had been fashioned in the 1770s by hammer-smith jewelers, who sliced silver coins in half so that each button was the head or tail of a coin. You could still read the dates. The fronts had initials engraved in them and the outlines of family crests. They were the oldest buttons anyone in Tryon had ever seen. But no one was of a mind to keep one. They didn't want to be haunted by ghosts, and there's no surer way to bring a ghost into your house than to steal from a grave.

The preacher said the appropriate words. Fayette sang a hymn. Bill played guitar. Lanier tossed her rubber ball to within a few inches of Ambrose's grave, which contained the remains of both his body and his head.

Ambrose came by after supper that night. His head was in place, and he was smiling so hard Fayette thought it might fall off. Bill invited him to come in and sit by the fire. Ambrose stepped inside but said he didn't have time to sit. He was in a hurry to get some rest.

"If you have a piece of paper, I'll draw you a map of where I buried my barrels of gold and silver coins," he said. "I'd like you two to have it all."

"We'll take none of that," Fayette said. "That money belongs to your kin. It's not for us."

"Hold on a second, honey," Bill said.

"It's devil money," Fayette insisted. "It won't bring us anything we really want."

"Well, then, what do you want?" Ambrose asked. "I've been dead for more than 150 years, and I've been an active ghost. I haven't had a wink of sleep. You can't shut your eyes when you don't have them with you. So I have made many connections on this side of life, and I have considerable influence. Whatever you want, I'll try to get for you."

"I want my granny's singing voice," Fayette said.

Ambrose nodded, kicking at the rubber ball with his

right foot, rolling it across the floor. Lanier had it in her mouth in a flash.

"I'll talk to your grandmother. I'm sure she won't mind if you have her singing voice. I'll bring it to you tonight while you're asleep. You can try it out in the morning.

"Now," Ambrose said, "what is it you want from a grateful ghost, Mr. Johnson?"

Bill knew right off.

"I want to play Hawaiian guitar," he said. "I want to be able to play that hula music."

It was all the rage, but no matter how hard Bill had tried to teach himself, he couldn't make his fingers do it right.

Ambrose thought a minute.

"I can find someone on my side of life who plays Hawaiian guitar. I'll bet you I can. I imagine there's a guitar stuck here or there that someone dead isn't using any longer. It'll be here in the morning when you get up, sir.

"Now, if you two don't mind my saying goodnight," Ambrose said, "I'll take my leave."

Lanier lowered her head and raised it quickly up, letting the rubber ball go at just the right time to make it bounce high to the ghost. Ambrose caught it in one hand.

"I suppose I was forgetting someone," Colonel Ambrose Mills said, clearing his throat. He couldn't get over being able to do that.

He squatted on his boot heels, and Lanier rushed forward, her tail wagging.

"I have you to thank the most," Ambrose said in dog

words. "Whatever it is I can do for you, Miss Lanier, just say the word, and I'll do my best. That's a gentleman's promise."

Lanier supposed she had enough sticks in her pile by the pond. She didn't really need any more of those. And any person she'd ever met could be trained to throw the ball for her, if she worked at it.

She'd had a real fine time finding that head in the creek bottom. It had been her favorite thing of late. That and finding the bones that went with it. No, finding the head was the best part. She really liked sticking her face in water.

"Anything?" Lanier asked. "Anything at all?"

"Nothing means more to me than your having found my head."

"In that case, I'd like to do the whole thing again," Lanier said.

Ambrose quit smiling. He handed Lanier her ball. Happiness for a Black Labrador Retriever is doing the same thing over again. Colonel Ambrose Mills should have thought of that before he asked a Labrador, or any dog that was half Labrador and half something bigger, to retrieve his head for him. His only excuse was that it was hard to think of everything when you didn't have your head with you.

The Revolutionary War ghost of Wilderness Road kept his promises.

When Fayette woke up in the morning, she stood by the window and sang a hymn her granny knew by heart. It was her grandmother's voice. Fayette recognized it immediately. Tears came into her eyes while she sang. It was prettier and sweeter than any song she had sung before. She tried another one, and her grandmother's voice was there. Fayette couldn't stop crying. It was better than Christmas.

Bill found a metal resonator guitar propped along the wall by the fireplace. It had a chrome bar held across the frets by a leather strap. He picked the guitar up and gave it a lick, and hula music came out, just like he'd always wanted to play. He grinned madly and kept playing.

Lanier rushed outside as soon as the door was open, leaving her rubber ball in the middle of the rug, where she'd been sleeping. She found a skull in the creek bottom, right where it had been before, and dug it up. It would be a few years yet before Colonel Ambrose Mills had any real rest.

Buddy

Jackson, Mississippi

Dogs can be as peculiar as people. Audrey Gerrin's dog, Buddy, was devoted from an early age to the habit of presenting her with a daily gift. Audrey's peculiarity was to accept what Buddy gave her as if she had been waiting all her life for a badly chewed extension-cord plug from the neighbor's trash. Whatever Buddy brought to her made Audrey's day special.

Audrey was introduced to Buddy when she was seven years old. Penny Gerrin walked her daughter to school each morning and walked her home in the afternoon. The old man who lived in the house on the corner called them over that day with a greeting and a wave of his hand. The old man had a large backyard he never mowed. Far from it. He grew okra back there and planted corn. A tall stand of cane formed a natural fence across the back. Bushy, rangy plants were everywhere, with winding paths cut through to a shed with a chicken coop on one side. The old man didn't have any chickens. They weren't allowed in town.

He had cats. Sitting in a rocking chair on the rock porch he'd built himself, he teased his cats with a piece of rag tied to the end of a long stick. Audrey liked seeing his cats. They had good motors that came on with a steady purring when you petted them.

Earlier that year, the old man had told Audrey it was his birthday. He was eighty-six. Audrey's mother baked a cake with Audrey's help, and the young girl carried it to the old man's house while the pan was still warm.

Audrey enjoyed stepping up on the old man's porch while Penny Gerrin commented on the weather. One end of the porch was entirely covered, all the way to the roof, with morning-glory vines. The other end was honeysuckle. Audrey liked the front porch and saying hello to his cats, but she was afraid of the old man's backyard. Afraid, that is, until he said the magic word.

"Hello, sir," Audrey said, standing in front of him, sticking out her hand.

The old man leaned forward in his chair and shook

Audrey's hand. He asked how her day at school had been. After she told him, the old man said he had a surprise for her, if she had time to see it.

"Puppies," he said. "I told them about you, and I believe they are waiting to see you now."

When Audrey learned there were puppies in a small chicken-wire pen attached to the old man's shed out back, she was no longer afraid of his backyard. Before her mother might say anything to keep her from it, Audrey was running around the side of his house on her way to the chicken coop. She dropped to her knees and stuck her fingers through the wire. Buddy was the first to greet her.

"They were inseparable," Penny Gerrin recalled. "Buddy was Audrey's constant companion. I couldn't walk Buddy on a leash when Audrey went to school. He would refuse to leave once she went into the building. I'd end up carrying him home, and he'd try to squirm out of my arms all the way."

When they moved to the new house in Jackson, Audrey was nine years old. She didn't want to move because it meant she had to change schools. There were no other girls her age in the new neighborhood.

"She probably would have refused to move at all, except the new house had a very large yard," Penny said. "I told her Buddy needed more room."

As soon as the car door was open on moving day, Buddy leapt free from Audrey's arms, and the two of them dashed into the backyard. There were trees. She could have a swing, her mother told her. And maybe a tree house, if she promised to be very, very careful.

35

36   *Buddy*

"Buddy was always digging up something," Penny recalled. "You never knew what he was after. Audrey hadn't come into the house yet, hadn't seen her new room, when Buddy found her a gift."

He raced to a spot in the yard as if he had a map. It was by the biggest tree in back. Buddy barked when he found the place to dig and then went at it. Sometimes, it was nothing more than an old walnut a squirrel had buried, but Buddy always found something. What he uncovered this time was a girl's bracelet.

"No telling how long it had been there," Penny said. "It was a simple gold chain with a small, round plate in the middle etched with the initial **M**. The clasp was broken off, but the rest of it cleaned up nicely. Audrey treasured it. I said I could fix it so she could wear it, but Audrey didn't want to wear it. She put it in a little cedar jewelry box we'd bought her when we went to Biloxi. It was her first piece of real jewelry."

Buddy slept in Audrey's bed. Penny didn't know if it was the result of their being in a new house or not, but she found Buddy curled up on the living-room sofa when she got up in the morning. It was the first time since he'd been housebroken that Buddy hadn't spent the night in Audrey's room.

Soon, Buddy wouldn't go into her room at all. After a week of this, Penny asked her daughter about it.

"Mildred doesn't want him there," the nine-year-old said.

"Who's Mildred?"

"My friend," Audrey replied, as if the answer were obvious. "She lived here before we did."

Penny had noticed that Audrey was spending less time with Buddy. Buddy noticed, too. No animal on earth can look as deeply disappointed as a dog. He'd lie outside the door to her room and mope.

Eventually, he became glum. Audrey spent more and more time locked in her room playing with Mildred, who her parents assumed was an imaginary friend. Penny talked to her husband about the situation, and he said it was a natural reaction to Audrey's having changed schools in the middle of the year. It would take her awhile to make new friends.

Penny tried to entertain Buddy, but he wasn't interested. He'd been shunned by Audrey, and he didn't understand it.

"I noticed Audrey wasn't getting enough sleep," Penny said. "She was always tired, and I was worried about this. At the time, I hadn't figured it out. In my daughter's mind, the bracelet Buddy had found in the yard belonged to Mildred. It was her initial that was engraved on it.

"We'd been there three weeks. Everything was unpacked, and it was time I started working in the yard. I made Buddy go with me while I raked leaves. He was just the saddest thing. Usually when you were in the yard with him, he ran every which way. When you raked leaves, he was right in the middle of them. Now, he just stood between me and the house, turning his head from time to time to see if Audrey was coming outside."

Buddy understood. Mildred was a ghost. He could see her. She lived in Audrey's room. Mildred didn't like Buddy, not one bit.

As Penny moved to the big tree with her rake and basket, Buddy came alert. He raced to join her.

"Buddy came right to where I was raking and started digging. I managed to get some of the leaves out of the way. Then I went to the other side of the tree. Buddy barked at something in the ground and kept digging. Then the leaves sort of danced at my feet. They moved around.

"I thought for a second there was something under the old leaves. They'd move, and they'd stop again. Like something was running through them. I raked them up in a hurry. I emptied the basket on top of the other leaves for my husband to burn and went inside. I called Buddy, but he was still digging. I left him out there.

"Buddy came in when my husband came home. They were both tired and hungry. I didn't like Buddy digging the yard, but at least he was doing something besides lying around the house looking sad all the time.

"That night when I went to bed, it came to me. The initial on the bracelet. I got right up and went to Audrey's room. Buddy watched me when I walked through the living room, but he didn't come along. I turned on the light. She was in bed, but she wasn't sleeping.

"When I told her I wanted to talk to her about Mildred, she started giggling, like someone was tickling her. I asked her where the bracelet was, and she had it under her pillow."

Penny asked her daughter to tell her about Mildred.

"She's right here looking at you," Audrey said.

"We have to put the bracelet back."

"I know," Audrey said. "I'm tried of playing. But Mildred won't let me stop."

"Her parents moved, honey. Just like we did. She has to go to her other home now. Give me the bracelet."

Penny Gerrin put her clothes on while her husband snored in bed. She didn't want the bracelet in her house. She didn't want to meet Mildred, whoever she was, and she didn't want Mildred bothering her daughter any longer.

"I put my hard shoes on," Penny recalled. "I went to the garage and got a shovel. Buddy came outside with me. I went to where we had the trash barrel, and I started digging. I dug for quite a bit. The whole time, Buddy was running around the big tree in the dark, barking and having a lively old time.

"I put that gold bracelet in the ground and covered it up. When I was through, I moved the trash barrel on top of it to keep Buddy, or anyone else, from digging it back up.

"Buddy was still running around that old tree when I was done, and I thought maybe he'd gone crazy. He came inside, though, when I called him to."

When Penny got up in the morning to fix breakfast, Buddy wasn't on the couch. He was back in Audrey's room.

"They were pals again," Penny said. "Audrey never mentioned Mildred, and I never found out who she was, although I could have asked around and maybe found out. I think all the people who lived in the house are listed on the deed somewhere. I just didn't want to know. I didn't want to know how she died. And maybe she was still alive, an older woman living somewhere else who got to be a girl

again when she was at our house.

"Buddy was a real happy dog after that, happier than before. And he was active right off. As soon as Audrey left for school, I let him out the back, and he raced to that tree. He was acting real peculiar, and he stayed out there all morning.

"When I went outside to see if he was eating crazy mushrooms or something, he was sitting on the concrete stoop, kind of rolling over on his back and putting his paws in the air. When I went out there, he rolled right over and raced to that tree again, barking his head off.

"This will sound funny, I know. But you could see he was playing with something. He was chasing around that tree, and every once in a while he'd roll up in a ball, like it had caught him. He was downright joyous about it. Then Buddy would take off in circles again, like something was chasing him."

Penny walked to the tree. She walked around it. Buddy stopped running. He sat down and looked at her.

"He walked over to that hole he'd dug and rooted around for a minute and brought me a gift," Penny said. "I took it from Buddy. It was another piece of chain, but this one was thick, old chain with some rotted leather stuck to it. It had a metal tag on it that looked like brass. I took it inside and washed it off. It was a dog tag with the words *City of Jackson* stamped on it, and the date, *1924*."

Buddy had found his own ghost to play with.

Granny Dollar

Mentone, Alabama

Granny Dollar was born Nancy Callahan in 1826. Her father was William Callahan, a Cherokee giant, believed to have been seven feet tall. Nancy learned to love the mountains at an early age.

When soldiers began to round up the Cherokee for removal from their homes in North Carolina, Tennessee, Georgia, and Alabama, Nancy's family fled into the nearby mountains. They hid in caves with others who sought to escape forced evacuation on the Trail of Tears. Born into a farmer's family, Nancy soon learned new skills. Along with other children, she scavenged food at night. She found lookout perches among the rocky mountain outcrops where she could spy on the uniformed militia who routinely conducted searches throughout the area.

Once the homes of the Cherokee were controlled by the government and the Trail of Tears was completed, military activity ended. What Indians remained were left in poverty in mountain gorges no one cared to occupy.

William Callahan moved his family to Georgia in the 1850s and began a delivery service. Atlanta wholesalers paid him a small fee to haul wagonloads of merchandise to small country stores. He saved his money to one day buy land upon which the Callahans might once again be farmers.

Nancy worked with her father, driving a wagon on the Georgia back roads. Unlike him, she didn't dream of being a farmer. In the mountains, she'd learned to love all things wild. She longed to return.

Though overage, William Callahan signed up for the Confederate Home Guard when the War Between the States came to Georgia. He was killed in the Battle of Atlanta. Nancy shed the lowlands and returned to the lower tip of the Appalachian Mountains in northeast Alabama. She built a cabin in an area of Lookout Mountain that is today the town of Mentone.

Lookout Mountain is an eighteen-mile-long strip of rocky plateau known for its scenic beauty and clear spring water. Mentone is a tourist town with a population of fewer than five hundred people. It is rumored to be the coldest spot in Alabama. The Cloudmont Ski Resort is nearby. Summer camps have popped up in the area, as have bed-and-breakfast establishments proud to offer their patrons the luxury of cool mountain evenings in the dread heat of Southern summers.

Lori Lovett, a counselor at a girls' summer camp on the eastern brow of Lookout Mountain, had heard all the stories of Granny Dollar around the campfire at night. Or so she thought. Lori attended the camp for several summers before becoming a counselor there. Granny Dollar was a local legend. It was said her ghost, in the company of a ghost dog, could be seen walking the woods at night.

Summer-camp activities on Lookout Mountain include horseback riding along scenic wooded trails. Her first year as a counselor, when she was sixteen, Lori led the six girls in her cabin through the woods on horseback. The horses were gentle mounts, accustomed to their route. But Lori's horse was acting up.

It stopped in the middle of the trail and turned sideways. Soon, it became clear to Lori that the horse wasn't going anywhere. She dismounted and tried walking in front of it, tugging on the reins. Nothing doing.

The other girls stopped in their tracks, their horses content to rest for a spell. The campers likely assumed that the stop was a regular part of the trail ride and that the counselor was going to point out to them some feature of the habitat, another large stand of rhododendron, perhaps.

Lori left her horse and walked the trail ahead. She managed a few steps before she saw the reason her mount had stopped. There were bees on the trail. They lay on the ground like a small, undulating piece of carpet. And they were moving, as a group, off the trail into a shallow between two trees. Lori watched their progress with rapt attention. She'd never seen bees on the ground before.

"Just a minute!" she yelled over her shoulder to the young campers.

Lori followed the bees. There was a dip in the ground, a smooth area, and the bees soon covered it entirely. She thought they might be drinking something from the ground. The bees fumbled in a large mass, spreading out. Two arms grew from one side of the main mass of bees. Near one end of the main group, a small group formed into a neck and a larger, nearly squared-off end. That's when Lori saw what it was. Her breath caught. Hairs raised on the back of her neck. Goose bumps covered her legs. A narrow trail of bees curled from the other end, concluding in a tip.

The bees had formed the shape of a dog on the ground. A big dog.

They stayed that way, holding their places. Lori backed up carefully. She wanted to run. She wanted to show her girls the bees but was afraid one of them might get stung. Lori walked back to her horse, wondering why no one had ever told her about bees camping on the ground. She looked over her shoulder.

Lori heard them move. As a group, they took flight, buzzing loudly. She turned and watched. If the cloud of bees came toward her, she would scream. Instead, the large swarm of bees flew away between the trees and was gone.

"What is it?" one of the girls asked once Lori returned to the group. "What's going on?"

Lori didn't want to tell the young girls there was a huge swarm of bees in the woods. They might never leave their cabin again. Or worse, they might call their parents and ask to be taken home.

"Nothing," she said.

She climbed into the saddle with a practiced swing of her right leg and clicked her tongue. Her horse moved willingly.

"Right over there is the old foundation of a pioneer cabin," Lori said loudly in her tour guide's voice. "It's where Granny Dollar lived. I thought you could see it from the trail, but I couldn't find it."

<hr/>

Lori learned the rest of the story of Granny Dollar when she talked to the camp's owners that evening. They had lived on Lookout Mountain their entire lives.

Nancy Callahan became Granny Dollar in 1903, when, at the age of seventy-seven, she married Nelson Dollar, a few years her junior. It was her first marriage. And her last. Nancy buried her husband in 1923. He was ninety-two. She was ninety-seven. For her ninety-fifth birthday, Nelson had given his wife a puppy she named Looksee. Except for her dog, Granny Dollar lived alone in her cabin during her last years, operating a business that had come to her late in life, as had her beloved companion, Looksee.

Looksee was an inelegant pup. His legs were too long, his feet too big, and his neck too thick. He had flop-over ears and the curiosity of a stranger plopped down in a brand-new world—Granny Dollar's cabin. He looked at everything, turning his head sideways and then turning it back, without ever taking his eyes off what he was seeing. Many of the things he looked at Granny couldn't see at all. She began to wonder if her house was full of fairies.

The puppy grew. It changed into a large dog. It became, to both Nancy's and her husband's surprise, a Great Dane.

"It was just a puppy I bought from a man who had them in his car at the store in town," Nelson told his wife. "He never said what kind it was."

Great Danes are born with the personality of Minnie Pearl. Their one mission in life is to say "Howdy." They are the official greeters of the dog world. And no creature attending the party of life is ignored, no matter how large or small. Great Danes have been known to lower their necks, bring their big noses to a trail of ants on a sidewalk, and, looking at each one, follow it to its end. They show no reticence in loping across a field to greet a horse, saying a personal hello. The dogs are likewise perfect companions in a roomful of cats.

Great Danes' sight is more sensitive than their ability to scent. The famous poised alertness of the dogs is attributed to the fact that they are "sighting" at all times. Because of this, many people have come to believe that Great Danes possess second sight, an ability to see ghosts. The dogs can

49

also come stock-still in the middle of the yard and watch a cricket climb a tree. Owners never know exactly what their Great Danes are looking at. Their quizzical and fixated stare is at times comical, especially when it is the opinion of the owner that the pet is staring into empty space.

Great Danes see the little things, and they see the things far away. They also adore other creatures. They won't pass up the opportunity to introduce themselves to a frog.

Looksee was no exception. He seemed completely unaware of his size. He befriended a mouse that came onto the porch one day by lowering himself to eye level with the little mammal and pushing it along with his nose. When the mouse tired of the game, it ran willy-nilly off the edge of the porch and back under the porch boards. Looksee righted himself and hurried to come along, falling off the porch with an exaggerated lack of grace. Then he tried to push himself under the boards where the mouse had gone. He barked.

"You chasing another ghost, Looksee?" Granny Dollar stood in the front door with a basket on her arm. Together, she and Looksee walked down the trail from her cabin to gather wild herbs.

Nancy was known as "Granny" throughout the area of Lookout Mountain not simply for her age. She was also a healer and a seer, a personality known throughout the southern Appalachians as a granny woman. In her younger years, she had routinely provided the service of a midwife.

Perhaps because she was Cherokee, people believed Granny Dollar could tell the future. She allowed it. In fact, she made a little bit of money charging folks a nickel to read their palms. She was good with a knife and whittled whistles from green wood, which she gave to every child she met. She and Nelson sold vegetables from their garden and traded mountain herbs at the local store. They got by, but there was never much money in their lives.

When Nelson died, Granny about quit doing anything. Looksee, of course, accustomed to activity, began to misbehave. He'd stand at the door of Granny Dollar's and bark, trying to get her up and moving. But the most she'd do was come out on the cabin porch and sit in a chair and watch the yard with Looksee at her feet.

The dog was heavily bored by this new routine. The porch was too small a world for Looksee. There were chipmunks in the woods to greet. There were blacksnakes that needed to be looked at very closely to see which end was which. There were grasshoppers waiting to leap. Still, the dog was loyal. He wouldn't leave the yard if Granny Dollar didn't.

Then, one day, a honeybee landed on his nose. It tickled, but it was awfully cute. The Great Dane went cross-eyed looking at it. The bee flew a circle around his head.

Granny Dollar noticed it.

"That's good luck," she said, "a bee buzzing around your head."

Looksee twisted his neck to the left and right, snapping his head up, then down, his eyebrows dancing as he watched the bee's circling flight. It was his lucky day.

When the bee took off, Looksee jumped up to follow

it. He loped to the edge of the yard. The honeybee kept going. It flew higher than you might expect. Looksee barked.

Granny Dollar pulled herself from her chair. Was it that bee he was after?

"Oh, all right," she said, stepping into the yard. "You may as well go after it."

The big dog glanced back once, saw that she was coming along, and bolted after the bee. Great Danes love to run. Of course, they also run into things. Granny Dollar was worried Looksee would knock himself out running into a tree, if he kept his eye on the bee and got going good. If you know Great Danes, you know it wasn't an idle fret.

She hurried after him. *Why not?* she thought. Her legs still worked. *You get to be ninety-seven, you might as well use what you have that works.*

Looksee led her to a hive of bees in a tulip poplar tree. The tree leaned over a creek. Looksee was in the water staring up at the buzzing bees from that angle, then up on the bank getting a better look from there. Bees flew down to investigate. Looksee didn't mind. They gave him the once-over, head to tail, then flew back to the hive again. Looksee was happy to say hello to each one individually.

Granny Dollar knew what to do with her good fortune. Soon, she was selling wild honey from her cabin. Many people believed wild honey was better than honey harvested from commercial box-hives. Tourists came to Frank Caldwell's 116-room hotel in Mentone to enjoy mountain air and drink mineral-spring water. They rarely checked out without buying a jar of Granny Dollar's wild-comb honey.

Looksee made friends with the little buccaneers of buzz all along Lookout Mountain. Meeting bees was his favorite activity. Most of all, it was something he and Granny Dollar could do together. She was careful to harvest the honey judiciously, taking only a small portion on a visit. Bees had to live through the winter, too. And, now that Looksee knew how to get himself invited to a hive, it seemed like all the bees in Alabama were moving to Lookout Mountain.

"They must be thinking you keep the bears away," Granny Dollar told Looksee. "If you could grow wings, they'd have you come on inside and sit down for a biscuit and tea."

Granny Dollar died in January 1931. She was 105 years young. It was the beginning of the Great Depression, and she was buried without a marker in the local cemetery. Looksee wouldn't leave the cabin. He didn't know where Nancy was, but he was content to wait for her return. Neighbors brought food by and made sure the dog had water. They set it on the porch. Looksee wouldn't let anyone into the cabin. It was the only time in his life he refused to say hello to anyone.

Granny Dollar had no heirs. Gentlemen in white shirts and neckties in the court clerk's office discussed the ownership of her cabin and small tract of mountain land. By the time they decided it belonged to the county, there wasn't much left of Granny Dollar's cabin. Rumor had spread through the town that the old woman was rich. Nearly everyone else on Lookout Mountain was poor in 1931. Because of the Depression, tourists had stopped coming to the hotel. Tourism was the only economy to speak of in Mentone. Ruffians figured there was money in Granny Dollar's cabin, and they meant to get it.

One night not long after her passing, two men with guns showed up at the place. They opened the front door. This startled Looksee. He could tell instantly that something was amiss. He leapt at the men, came out the door, and, in his usual display of physical grace, slid across the porch and into the yard. He bounded to his feet and assumed a pose of attack, something he'd never done before. He snarled in earnest, baring his teeth. He growled.

One of the men shot Granny Dollar's Great Dane in the head. Looksee died quickly.

The robbers rushed inside the house, ready to ransack the cabin to find the granny woman's stash, the money she'd made selling wild honey the past several years. One of them had brought along a coal-oil lamp. He lit it and lengthened the wick. Light filled the room.

"Oh, my cow!" a robber said. Undulating swarms of bees covered the walls. There must have been a dozen hives inside the structure.

They backed cautiously from the room. Bees are calmer at night than they are in the daytime. The men stepped over Looksee's body and ran from the yard.

They came back two hours later with matches and a plan. Easing inside, one of them started a pitch fire in a pot on the floor, hoping to smoke the bees out.

It didn't work. Something went wrong with the flame, and the cabin caught fire. It burned to the ground.

Neighbors came by in the morning. Someone had shot the dog. They buried Looksee without ceremony in a low place in Granny Dollar's yard.

No one found her money. If she saved paper bills, they likely burned up in the fire. If she had her money in coins, as most people did in those years, it might still be buried somewhere around the place.

Lori knew the rest of the story. The ghost of a woman and her dog were seen frequently in the woods on Lookout Mountain. The sightings continued for years. Whenever the ghosts were seen, folks were apt to mention that both the woman and the dog seemed to be looking up into the trees. Annie Young of nearby Fort Payne believed she knew how to put the ghosts to rest. She took in contributions for a headstone for Granny Dollar's grave. A marker was erected in its proper place in 1973.

Of course, you'll have to ask the woodland honeybees on Lookout Mountain where the proper place to visit the dead might really be. They'll likely point you to a low dip in the woods alongside the mountain trail that once was the edge of Granny Dollar's yard.

Butterfly Dog

Knoxville, Tennessee

Linda Shockley was eleven years old when she had an accident on her bicycle one summer in the late 1970s. She fell and hit her head on the curb. She was knocked unconscious. Falling from one's bicycle is a relatively common affair among children. The effects of Linda's accident, however, were quite uncommon.

Unable to bring her to, Linda's mother rushed her daughter to the hospital, where she was treated in the emergency room, then quickly transferred to an intensive-care unit. Linda was in a coma. Specialists were called in. While there was nothing more than a lump on the side of the girl's head, her life was at stake.

"She must be watched carefully," the neurosurgeon told Linda's mother.

Internal bleeding was putting pressure on Linda's brain. If she did not regain consciousness, and if the swelling did not go down on its own, surgery would be required. The duration of Linda's coma could not be predicted.

Mrs. Shockley prayed. She held her daughter's hand and prayed her heart out.

Her prayers were answered. Within hours, Linda regained consciousness. The swelling went down. Two days later, she was released from the hospital.

Five years later, when Linda was sixteen, she attended an antiques show at the Knoxville Civic Auditorium with her mother. Linda had received a hope chest for Christmas. Mother and daughter were looking for something special to begin Linda's collection of items for her future household.

"We were hoping to find a bit of antique lace, perhaps a set of formal table napkins," Linda's mother recalled. "It was very warm in the building, and we were wearing our winter coats."

Linda had found a set of four antique silver napkin rings and was carefully examining them. Each napkin ring had been deeply etched with the outline of a small bouquet of flowers.

"These are nice," she said.

"They're very pretty," Mrs. Shockley agreed, "but you'll want more than four that match, don't you think?"

It would be difficult, if not impossible, to find matching napkin rings, Linda decided. She reluctantly set aside her interest in the set of four. She surveyed the auditorium to see where they might head next. At that instant, a pain shot through her head like a bullet.

Linda dropped to her knees. She was blinded by a sudden headache. It was more intensely painful than anything she could remember. And she was overcome with a feeling of nausea. Bent over on her knees, her eyes squeezed tightly shut, Linda held her hands to her face.

"What's wrong?" her mother said quickly, kneeling at her daughter's side.

"I have to throw up, Momma." Linda's eyes were still closed. Her head throbbed mercilessly.

"It's okay, honey. It's okay." Mrs. Shockley put her hand gently on her daughter's back.

"My head hurts," Linda mumbled. "My head hurts."

"It'll be okay, darling," Mrs. Shockley said, hoping that it would. "Do you want some water?"

The nausea passed. Despite the headache, Linda was relieved. She could think of nothing more humiliating than throwing up in public. The pain eased, and Linda removed her hands from her face.

Still on her knees, she opened her eyes. There were people everywhere. They were practically standing on top of her. They were crowded among the displays. A young lady in heavy makeup stood directly in front of Linda, staring at her. She carried a small dog under one arm. The woman wore a shimmering, beaded dress with black fringe that hit just above her knees. Her lips were dark red. Linda glanced down at the woman's shoes. They were black leather with rounded toes and thick, high heels. Black straps crossed over the woman's ankles. Linda had never seen shoes like that before. Behind the woman stood a young man in a tuxedo. He had dark, oiled hair that shone like patent leather. He said something to the woman, but Linda couldn't hear the words.

"Who are these people, Momma?"

There were many others milling around in funny costumes. It seemed to Linda as if she were on stage in the middle of a play. The people looked like actors to her.

Another pain slapped through her forehead, and she closed her eyes for a moment. When she opened them again, the dog wiggled loose from the woman's arms and jumped to the floor. It approached Linda and stood right at her knees. It was a funny-looking little dog, only ten inches high, with big, upright ears that looked like butterfly wings.

Linda bent forward and touched the dog gingerly with one hand. It was so small she thought it might be a child's toy. But it was real. It was also real friendly. It climbed into Linda's lap in an instant and licked her face.

The pain went away. The dog had a long tail that it never stopped wagging. The tail had a silky fringe of long, fine hair. Linda smiled a little.

She looked up at her mother. When she did, the dog

was gone. The people in funny costumes disappeared. Her headache was gone.

"I'm all right," she said.

"Are you sure? What was it, darling?" Mrs. Shockley helped her daughter stand up.

"I'm okay. It was just a headache. I forgot to eat or something."

"Maybe we should go," her mother suggested. "Let's get something for lunch. Are you sure you're all right now?"

Mrs. Shockley thought about the bicycle accident, remembering the excruciating hours her daughter had spent in a coma. No one had said a word about future side effects.

On the way to the car, Linda asked her mother about the people she'd seen.

"Was there a play in the auditorium, Momma? Did you notice if there was a play or something?" Perhaps the actors had walked through the antiques show during a rehearsal break.

"I don't think so, darling. Why do you ask?"

"All those people in funny clothes. What were they doing there?"

Mrs. Shockley didn't know. People were dressed every which way.

"And what about that little dog?" Linda asked. "Have you ever seen a little dog like that before?"

"What dog was that?" her mother wanted to know.

"The one that came over and licked my face."

"I didn't see a dog. I don't think they would let people

bring their pets to an antiques show."

"The little dog the woman in the beaded dress was holding. It jumped out of her arms." Linda paused. She stopped walking and stared at her mother. "You really didn't see it?"

Linda described the people and their clothes in greater detail on the ride home.

Mrs. Shockley smiled awkwardly. She hadn't seen the dog. She hadn't noticed the woman in the beaded dress either. Nor had there been anyone in a tuxedo.

"It sounds to me like you saw a flapper. You know, from the Roaring Twenties. It sounds like they were dressed up for something special."

Eventually, they came to the conclusion that Linda had seen ghosts. It was the only thing that made sense. Mrs. Shockley was convinced her daughter wasn't making up the experience. She'd been with her when it happened.

"I wonder if they had a formal dedication of a building there in the twenties," Mrs. Shockley said. "If there were several people dressed up like that, it had to be an event of some kind."

"They weren't all in formal wear, Momma. Some were just wearing funny clothes. You know, old-timey clothes. There were men with big pants, and they had hats on. And real clunky shoes."

"You think they came with the antiques?" Mrs. Shockley asked. "Maybe they were the people who owned some of those things. There was a lot of formal tableware."

"And the engraved silver," Linda added. "Some of it had initials on the handles."

Mrs. Shockley thought of the elaborately designed silver serving pieces displayed alongside an ornate crystal punch bowl and goblet set. They were the sort of things that would be used for a fancy party or formal gathering. Chills ran up her spine and tickled the hair at the back of her neck.

Mrs. Shockley scheduled her daughter for a CAT scan. It showed nothing out of the ordinary. Linda was given a prescription for migraine headaches and told to take one of the capsules whenever she felt a headache coming on.

"But I didn't feel it coming," Linda told the doctor. "It just happened all at once."

"Sometimes they do," the doctor said. "If you have additional migraines, you'll learn to recognize the signs."

"How often will I have them?" Linda was frightened by the prospect of severe and blinding headaches for the rest of her life.

The doctor told her it varied from individual to individual. Sometimes they went away altogether. Sometimes they increased in frequency.

"You're very young to have migraines," he said. "You may not have another one for years."

Mrs. Shockley had a question for the physician.

"Do people see things when they have migraines? I read the brochures you gave us, and it doesn't say anything about that."

"There may be a bright light that is sensed internally," he said. "It's a light that has been described as occurring behind the eyes and is usually associated with a sharp concentration of pain. Of course, a person suffering a migraine is very sensitive to light. It's probably a good idea to darken a room when the headache comes on."

Mrs. Shockley never bought another antique. It troubled her to think that the original owners of personal property might show up where the items were years later, long after their deaths.

Linda thought more and more about the little dog. It was the friendliest dog she'd ever met. Eventually, she found it in a book in the library. The dog in the picture looked exactly like the one that had licked her face when she knelt on the floor at the antiques show. It was called a Papillon, because of its large, upright ears.

Papillon is French for butterfly. And that's just what its ears had looked like to Linda. They'd looked like butterfly wings stuck to either side of the dog's head. She learned that the breed came in many color combinations. The one she'd seen was mostly white with a large brown blotch on its side and one at the end of its tail. It also was brown on its face and ears.

Linda discovered that some adult Papillons weigh as little as three pounds. Considered elegant dogs with exceedingly pleasant dispositions, the breed was described as friendly, happy, and eager to please. Papillons, she read, possess a hearty spirit, making them desirable human companions. The written description concluded with the statement that Papillons are hardy and usually long-lived.

Some more than others, Linda thought. She wondered if it were possible for dogs and people to live forever.

Linda Shockley never saw the woman in the beaded

dress or the man in the tuxedo again. And she never told anyone else about them. None of her friends knew that she had seen a roomful of ghosts at the Knoxville Civic Auditorium.

For her senior English project, Linda read *The Great Gatsby* by F. Scott Fitzgerald and wrote a research paper on American fashions in the 1920s. Because of her interest in the topic, she spent an extraordinary amount of time on the research and earned an A+ on the project. She mentioned in her paper that it was fashionable for Jazz Age women to carry a small dog to special occasions in the crook of an arm. A Continental Toy Spaniel, or Papillon, with large, erect ears was a popular choice.

On a particularly warm day in her high-school classroom, while the teacher droned on and on about something she wasn't really paying attention to, Linda experienced another blinding headache. It was as bad as before. Her prescription was at home in the medicine cabinet.

It had been well over a year since her painful, ghostly experience at the antiques show. Although she was sitting at her desk, she felt as if she were falling as her head imploded with pain. As before, she ended up on the floor, this time on her knees beside her desk. The room was hushed, and all eyes were turned to her. Linda didn't notice. She was too busy trying not to throw up.

Her eyes squeezed shut in pain, she buried her face in her hands.

Was she moaning out loud? She hoped not. The pain came in quick, hammering waves, and she couldn't move.

This time, the pain wouldn't go away.

Linda pried her hands from her face and squinted her eyes open. Old people were walking around the room. The little dog was right in front of her. It leapt onto her skirt. Its big, bright eyes were like lights. It licked her face, her chin. And the pain gradually subsided.

She put her fingers on the dog's silky coat. She touched its big ears. The pain was going away.

Thank you, she thought. It was the Papillon that made the pain stop. She understood that now. The little dog showed up when she needed it.

Linda could see now. She could open her eyes. Mr. Norris, her teacher, was hurrying toward her. The old people moved out of his way. Then they were gone.

"Linda, are you all right?"

Mr. Norris stood in front of her, and the little dog was gone.

She smoothed her hair with her hands and felt like a total geek. Happy to leave the classroom, Linda went to the school nurse, who made her lie down on the couch in her office. She put a wet washcloth on Linda's forehead. Linda swallowed two Tylenol.

The nurse called her mother. She asked Linda if this had happened before.

"No," Linda said. She didn't want word to get around school that she was a feeb. "I forgot to eat lunch today."

Mrs. Shockley arrived to pick up her daughter and drive her home.

"I'm just fine," Linda said. "I can drive my car."

"We'll get it later," her mother insisted.

Linda had to agree. She wasn't going back to Mr. Norris's class. That was for certain.

"Was it another migraine?" Mrs. Shockley asked Linda once they were in the car.

Now that they had a name for it, Linda feared her mother would never tire of throwing the word around.

"I don't think it's a migraine, Momma. I think it's something else."

"Oh?" Mrs. Shockley was surprised. "And what might that be?"

"I think it's my head remembering my accident. It is remembering when it hit the curb."

Mrs. Shockley didn't say anything.

"Well, that's what it feels like," Linda said. "It feels like my head hitting the curb, and I can't open my eyes."

Then she told her mother the rest of it.

"There were a bunch of old people in the room," she said. "I don't know who they were, just old people walking up and down the aisles between the desks. They were standing by the windows, looking at us."

Mrs. Shockley drove by rote. Her thoughts were elsewhere.

"What were they doing?"

"They weren't doing anything, Momma! They were just there, standing around. I think they wanted to sit in the desks, but we were already in them. They looked like they wanted to sit down."

Mrs. Shockley nodded. Linda went to classes in one of the oldest school buildings still in use in Knoxville.

"They went to school there," Mrs. Shockley finally said.

"They're students who have grown up."

"You mean they're students who have grown up and died?"

Mrs. Shockley wasn't sure.

"What were they wearing?" she asked.

"Nothing weird. Just clothes, I guess."

"No beaded dresses? No tuxedos?"

"No," Linda said. "Just clothes."

She couldn't believe what she had seen. But something else was going on. Her mother was acting funny. She knew something.

"The dog was there," Linda said. "The same dog from the antiques show. The Papillon."

Mrs. Shockley's face showed her reaction.

"What?" Linda said. "What aren't you telling me?"

Linda's mother eased the car into the driveway. The automatic garage door lifted, but she stopped the car outside in the daylight. She didn't want to drive into the close quarters of the garage.

"I was in the yard when it happened," Mrs. Shockley said without looking at her daughter.

She turned the car off. Linda waited for her to continue.

"I was calling for you to come home. It was time for supper. You were at the end of the block, and you came down the sidewalk when I called. You were on your bicycle, and you had a habit of making a big curve out into the street so you could coast straight up the driveway. That's what you did, Linda.

"You didn't see it, but there was a car behind you. The driver hit his horn when you pulled out into the street. He nearly ran into you. When he sounded the horn, you turned the bicycle into the sidewalk, and that's when you fell and hit your head."

"I don't remember a car," Linda said.

"It all happened very fast. You were eleven, Linda. You hit the curb with your head, and the next thing you remember was waking up in the hospital."

"Why didn't you tell me?"

"You didn't need to know. It wasn't his fault, Linda. It was yours. You were eleven years old and acting like an eleven-year-old. You're lucky the car didn't hit you. The driver had to swerve out of the way to avoid running over you."

"There's more," Linda said after a long pause. "There's something more."

"It was your father. He almost killed you, Linda. It scared him to death. I just couldn't tell you."

"He didn't mean to, Momma. Geez, you could have told me that."

"You were eleven years old, remember. Your father didn't want you to know. He felt horrible about it. He still does. When you were in a coma, he thought he'd killed you. He still hasn't forgiven himself."

Now that she was a senior in high school, Linda thought she understood. It was her fault that the accident happened. She'd be nicer to her father from now on. Linda put herself in his place. It must have been awful for him. She wondered if he had cried.

Linda placed her hand on the handle to open the door, but her mother touched her arm to stop her.

"Mrs. Ferguson across the street had company coming," Linda's mother said. "Her aunt from North Carolina was arriving that afternoon. In fact, she'd just pulled up in Mrs. Ferguson's driveway when I came outside to call you home. I waved at her. She was elderly, Linda. Mrs. Ferguson was still in the house. She didn't know her aunt was there yet. She'd just pulled up. Anyway, her aunt was having trouble getting out of her car. She had the car door open, and this little dog jumped out."

Linda knew the breed of the dog. She knew it in her heart.

"It was a Papillon," she said.

Mrs. Shockley nodded.

"The dog wanted to see you, Linda. It wanted to play. It had been in the car a long time, and when it saw you coming down our sidewalk, it started over here in a dash. That's when Mrs. Ferguson's aunt finally got out of the car. That's when I waved to her. Then I saw your father's car coming down the street. It all happened so fast."

Linda knew what happened. She knew why her mother had never told her, and she knew why her mother was telling her now. She started to cry. Her eyes filled with tears. Linda knew what happened, but she had to hear it to be sure.

"When your father swerved to miss you, darling, he ran over that little dog."

Mrs. Ferguson's aunt was heartbroken, but instead of rushing to her dog, she hurried across the street as best she could to check on Linda.

"She visited you in the hospital during those first hours," Mrs. Shockley told her daughter. "And even though her dog was dead, I think it came with her. When you were coming out of the coma, you asked if the dog was still there, if it was under the bed."

"I don't remember," Linda said. And yet she would never forget.

When Linda Shockley left home for college, she got a two-color tattoo of a butterfly high on her back, just behind her shoulder. It was the place on her body the tattoo artist told Linda it would hurt the least to have tattooed.

She can see it in a mirror when she turns sideways. Her Papillon is always there.

The headaches still come, but they are infrequent. The pain, she has learned, is temporary. Linda sees ghosts when she opens her eyes during an attack. She has learned to ignore them.

She never ignores the little, happy dog that shows up to lick her chin, to take the pain away. Linda always says a thank-you.

As for the tattoo, don't say anything to Linda's mother if you happen to see her. Linda hasn't told her yet.

Barking Creek

Yell County, Arkansas

Eva Marie Vann had her a dog long before she met Gallatin Pickett and married him. Her brother Emanuel, who had joined the army, brought home a gift for his sister the Christmas when Eva Marie was seventeen. It was a dog he called a Round Head. We currently know the breed as Boston Terrier. He was a little black dog, but he was white, too.

He had a white stripe in the middle of his face, a white breast and collar, and white at each of his four feet.

She named her dog Toro because he looked like a miniature bulldog to her. Whenever Eva Marie talked to her dog, he would stand up on his hind legs and dance in a circle.

"He's preaching back at me when he does that," she said.

Eva Marie taught school in rural Yell County, in a one-room clapboard building on the road between Onyx and Aly, Arkansas. It was a rugged landscape of rocky hilltops cut by mountain creeks. The area, part of the Ouachita National Forest today, has no soil worth farming. Maybe one or two short rows of corn can find standing room up close to somebody's house—enough for "squeezins," anyway.

The people who live there raise mainly chickens and pigs. And a litter of children now and then. The rocky hillsides are content to cover themselves with trees. Dogwoods light up the shady places with white flowers in spring. Redbuds grow like weeds. Foxglove is a common wildflower throughout the woods, as are, in more sunny spots, larkspur, coreopsis, purple cone, and partridge pea. Yell County, Arkansas, is a pretty place to live.

Eva Marie lived in a two-room house her father and brothers had built for her in a shady mountain cove. Chameleon lizards, able to change their color to either brown or green, posed from time to time on the lichen-covered rocks near her house. She had her own creek. It ran at a slant through the trees alongside the path to her house. When

Eva Marie was living there, the creek didn't have a name.

Gallatin Pickett was a gambling man. The only thing he raised in Yell County was the bid. He wasn't interested in anything for long, unless he could bet on it or against it. In the short run, he was interested in Eva Marie. Folks said he'd be lucky to catch her. He bet them he would.

Eva Marie guessed she was a gambler, too. She gambled on marrying Gallatin, who swore many things besides "for better or for worse." He swore he would never ask Eva Marie to give up teaching unless she wanted to. That was the foremost thing. He swore he'd be happy living in her house, too, in her hollow alongside the creek without a name. He didn't have a house of his own. And Gallatin swore he wouldn't gamble anymore.

He kept the first three of those promises right well.

Eva Marie was a pretty woman who was well respected at church. Her status as the schoolteacher meant a lot to both her and her family. The only thing she loved more than teaching school and hearing preaching was Toro.

Gallatin never swore anything about the dog. He swore *at* it. Once he moved into his wife's house, Toro moved outside. This grieved Eva Marie, but she'd made her oath, too, for better or for worse, and in the eyes of God and man alike, she meant to stick to it. She took Toro to school with her, so he wouldn't have to be outside all the time. At night, Toro slept under the porch.

A hunting hound came through her cove one night, just passing by. Toro shot out from under the porch and lit into the dog. He never knew how small he was. Boston Terriers are feisty fellows and won't run away from anything. He got a bite in on the hound about the time the hound got a bite on him.

Toro wouldn't let go. The hound bit Toro's hind leg off at the knee, as much from fear as from true aggression. Toro still wouldn't let go. The hound spun in a circle, hollering like hounds do, trying to throw Toro free. Toro wouldn't let go until Eva Marie came out of the house with a broom and clobbered the hound a few times hard on the head. With reinforcements like Eva Marie backing him up, Toro let loose of his bite and was flung off.

The hound skedaddled.

Eva Marie cried something awful when she saw Toro's hind leg was for the most part missing. She sewed up what remained.

Undaunted, the little dog went about his business on three legs for the rest of his days.

Gallatin couldn't stand to look at the three-legged dog. He started calling the dog Stump. Eva Marie hated the word so much that she began to hate her husband every time he said it. *Stump, Stump, Stump. Hate, hate, hate.*

Looking at a dog with three legs every time he went in or out of the house drove Gallatin crazy, and he turned mean. He started gambling again. He played cards in a hunting shack with men who met there for the purpose. There's a saying in Arkansas about a man like Gallatin who plays poker and can't quit until he loses. They say a man like that has been pokered bald.

First, they pokered him for the hat off his head. Then he lost his hair.

Gallatin gambled away all the money they had. He gambled away his comb. He was bald broke when he came home to Eva Marie the first night it came cold. She wanted her dog in the house. If Gallatin was going to gamble, then she wanted her dog back.

Gallatin couldn't be swayed. He said he'd cut off Toro's other leg if that dog came inside the door.

"See how he gets around after that," he said. "I'd think you'd want a dog that can stand up."

Eva Marie worried over it all night until she came up with a plan to save herself and Toro from Gallatin. Religion was to be the cure. A married man in Arkansas can't say no when his wife tells him he's going to church with her. Especially if she's the one who brings home the poker money. Gallatin, as mean as he was, obliged.

There was preaching every third Sunday of the month, held at the schoolhouse where Eva was the teacher. This was before they built the church that burned down later and isn't there anymore.

Brother Charley Christmas was a hard-shell Baptist. A circuit preacher who came to Yell County once a month on a saddled mule, he wore long, white hair and a pair of brass-rimmed spectacles to read the Bible by. Words flowed freely from Brother Charley, the big, booming words of God. What came to him was also given freely, slipped into his hand at the close of services in the form of pennies, nickels, and dimes by whosoever felt moved or were by their own nature so inclined.

Brother Charley's method and purpose of preaching were

simple. He meant to save souls from everlasting fire while there was still time. And there wasn't enough time to go around.

"I want you to be saved, Gallatin," Eva Marie said. "It's all I ask. Once you've been saved, you can make your own choices. They'll be the right ones."

At the end of the preaching, Eva Marie's husband knelt in front of Brother Charley, who placed his hand on Gallatin Pickett's shoulder and told him he was saved. It was as sure as if it had been written down on paper and signed. Eva Marie cried while the last hymns were sung.

When they got home that night, Toro came out from under the porch. He hopped around in a circle on his one back leg to say hello. He could still jump pretty good for a dog with three legs. Eva Marie had him in her arms when Gallatin opened the door.

"Where you going with that crippled dog?" Gallatin asked. "You ain't bringing it inside."

Gallatin was saved, but he was just as mean as before. What he needed was baptizing, Eva Marie decided.

Nothing Eva Marie had seen before in the deep woods was so lovely as the place Brother Charley found for baptizing sinners. It was at the big hole on Reed Creek, a wide, clear pool fringed with ferns growing from carpets of moss. A little fall of water flashed over a ledge of rock at the pool's upper end. A person who went in that water came out clean.

Gallatin thought it was too cold a time of year to be immersed. But Brother Charley had baptized women and children through ice.

"No one is ever made ill by the performance of his religious duty," the preacher said.

Everyone from the church was there to participate in the proceedings. And many others attended besides, simply to enjoy the spectacle.

Gallatin stood in the water up to his waist, his teeth chattering, while Brother Charley Christmas placed one hand low on his back and the other across Gallatin's forehead. The preacher asked him some question, and Gallatin answered without hesitation in the appropriate manner. Then down he went.

As soon as the preacher let go of him, Gallatin dashed and splashed clean out of the water. Like most converts, he was shouting by the time he reached the bank. He was still shouting as he changed quickly into dry clothes behind a hastily fashioned brush shelter erected for the purpose of providing a moment's privacy. Gallatin continued shouting as he trotted all the way home.

He had the spirit, everyone agreed.

Eva Marie discovered within a short amount of time that Gallatin remained inclined to gamble and that he was still mean. She fixed a nice supper and told her husband it was time her dog should come indoors. It was November now.

"That puppy lived with me before I ever met you," she said.

Gallatin said no.

"Toro lived in this house, my very own house that my kin built for me, before I met you, Gallatin Pickett!" She set the plates on the table.

Gallatin said the dog wasn't coming inside. Not that night. Not Christmas. Not ever.

"That dog is one of God's creatures!" she shouted. "And he's missing a leg. He can't curl up proper without it. He's coming inside tonight."

"Over my dead body," Gallatin mumbled, his mouth full of Eva Marie's fine cooking.

She heard him clear enough. Eva Marie had yet to sit down to eat with him and decided maybe she wouldn't. She walked into the other room while Gallatin was gobbling away at his supper. She returned with his rifle. Eva Marie shot her husband point-blank in the upper middle of his back.

Gallatin Pickett slumped forward in a hurry, filling his plate with blood. Blood spilled onto the table in leaps. Then he lifted himself out of that chair and took to hollering something fierce. His chair fell over sideways. Gallatin staggered across the room, banged out the front door, crossed the porch, and sat down on the step, still yelling his fool head off.

Toro came out and danced in a lopsided circle around the yard. He started barking and wouldn't stop. *Bark, bark, bark.* Gallatin wouldn't stop hollering. *Bark, bark, bark.* Hollering and yelling and screaming. *Bark, bark, bark.*

Now that her husband, as mean as he was, had been properly saved and rightfully baptized by a hard-shell Baptist preacher, Eva Marie figured Gallatin was going straight to heaven. You could bet on it. But she had to finish killing him first.

She dropped the single-shot rifle and found the hunting knife. Eva Marie rushed outside where her husband sat with a hole through him, hollering.

She started stabbing at him, all over and deep as she could.

Bark, bark, bark. Stab, stab, stab.

Gallatin quit hollering.

Bark. Stab.

Eva Marie went back inside, washed up a bit, and split her supper with Toro, who was very happy to be back. He stood to dance but, having only one leg back there, fell over fairly quickly. Eva Marie thought it was the cutest trick.

The sheriff of Yell County came out to see Eva Marie. She told him just what might have happened. She and Gallatin might have been getting ready to go hunting the next morning, and the two of them sort of tripped over each other in an accident. The gun went off, and when she tried to help him up, she could have plumb forgot the hunting knife was in her hand.

"What happened to that dog's leg?" the sheriff asked.

"Coonhound bit it off. Ain't he the saddest little thing?"

Brother Charley Christmas preached a fine funeral. Religion, like Toro's legs, comes in threes. Salvation, baptism, and Christian burial.

Eva Marie Pickett never married again. Her house, its windows long ago broken out, still stands in the overgrown woods along Barking Creek. Someone took the back door, but everything else is just as it was when she died and they carried her body away for burial behind the little church that burnt down and isn't there anymore.

People say there's yet a plate at the table where Gallatin Picket sat to eat his last supper. Hunters who use the house for temporary quarters in deer season verify this fact. One night a year, in November, on the anniversary of Gallatin Pickett's death, the plate fills up with fresh blood. It fills up with blood and overflows, there is so much of it. Then the chair falls over. You can watch it happen if you're lucky enough to be there on the anniversary of his death.

When the front door bangs open and shut at the hand of what surely is a ghost, a little dog that isn't there starts barking. He barks all night and doesn't stop. Coonhounds won't come near the place.

The Silver Locket

Belleview, Georgia

Magic has long been associated with both the hair and the tooth of a hound. The *Edinburgh Weekly Scotsman* of August 5, 1899, reported a trial of a woman of Holm village, near Stornoway, who was believed to be in possession of the tooth of a fairy's dog. Kate Campbell MacCaskill was charged with a breach of the peace upon the complaint of a Mrs. Mackay, who gave her testimony in Gaelic.

Mrs. Mackay claimed that Kate had said she would use the peculiar properties of the dog's magic tooth by placing it down the chimney and causing Mrs. Mackay's house to go up in fire. She further charged that Kate had threatened her immediate destruction if she told anyone that Kate possessed the tooth.

The sheriff asked the witness if the tooth was that of an animal. It was. The court further learned that the tooth possessed curative powers, that water into which it was dipped could be used to heal the sick. Even holding the tooth in one's hand could produce an immediate cure of any ailment.

Mrs. Mackay testified that, ten years earlier, she had held the tooth in her hand and had paid "an old wife" one shilling for the privilege.

Alexander Stewart, a resident of Holm village, testified that he had seen the tooth thirty years ago but could not say where it was now. His mother had rented it from "an old wife" and had shown it to her son. Stewart described the tooth as larger than a man's tooth, one end of it red, the other ending in decay. It was the tooth of a dog, in his opinion, the tooth of a dog that had commingled with fairies.

Another witness testified that she had paid a fee to use the tooth to cure her cattle many years earlier. The cattle were made to drink water in which the tooth was dipped. It cured them. It was the belief of this witness, and that of the others, that the original owner of the hound's tooth was Kate MacCaskill's great-grandfather, now deceased.

Kate MacCaskill was called as a witness in her own defense. She agreed that there had been words between herself and Mrs. Mackay, but nothing that amounted to a breach of the peace. Mrs. Mackay had been twitting her about the tooth, and Kate thought it was time to say something on her own behalf to her offender. Yes, Kate did say that if she had the tooth, Mrs. Mackay would be the first person she would kill with it. But Kate did not have the tooth and could not say where it was now.

The sheriff asked Kate if she knew how her great-grandfather had come into possession of the tooth. She answered that late one night when her great-grandfather was coming home from Stornoway, something met him on the road, asked of him a favor, and gave him the tooth in return. She did not know the favor granted, but believed it was the turning of a large stone that had tumbled into the path of a spring. Kate was asked whether she knew if her great-grandfather had taken any strong drink that night. She did not know. Upon further questioning, she confessed that she did not know for certain that it was a fairy who met her great-grandfather on the road on the night in question.

The testimony concluded. After brief deliberation, the sheriff rendered his verdict that the case seemed to him to be a neighbors' squabble, and nothing more. He also noted that Mrs. Mackay had migrated to Holm from the other side of the island only thirteen years prior. The select and exclusive community in Holm resisted her intrusion. The sheriff, Lord Campbell, found the charge against Kate unproven. In closing, he severely admonished the accused, his sister, for her abusive and offensive language. He offered a few more words of advice as to the manner in which people of the township should conduct themselves toward one another.

<hr />

Nearly fifty years prior to this trial, a twelve-year-old girl in Talbot County, Georgia, had a very different experience with a dog's tooth. It did not burn down the house. Rather, it ignited a strange fire within the young girl's soul.

Emily Burt was born July 29, 1841, on the family plantation near Belleview, a few miles southeast of Woodland, Georgia. Her father was well off, and Emily experienced a relatively carefree childhood.

The family considered her twelfth birthday a special one. She received a silver locket engraved with her monogram, and a local artist was hired to paint her portrait.

Emily adored the locket. Her initials had been facet-etched into the silver face by a jeweler. At the center, a deeply engraved design of a flower sparkled like diamonds. Emily was permitted to keep the locket in her room. She was not allowed to wear it out of the house. When she put it on, it made her feel different. She wore it proudly, posed stiffly in her best dress, while her portrait was painted.

"Your eyes are emeralds," the artist told her.

Emily smiled.

"I've never mixed this shade of green before," he said as

much to himself as to Emily. "Hold still!"

Emily quit smiling.

"Please turn your head back toward the window. Just a little. There, that's it."

Emily did her best to hold perfectly still. It wasn't easy.

"Eyes are like roses. They must be done with great care," the artist said.

Emily never thought of herself in the same way again. Her face was emeralds and roses. That was very pretty indeed. She wore diamond-cut silver on her neck.

The artist also painted a picture of Emily's mother. And one of her father, too.

A party was held when the portraits were done. Supper was served on the lawn. Emily was permitted to wear her locket among the small throng of guests, mostly cousins, aunts, and uncles. She was even allowed to drink coffee with her cake. Emily put four servings of sugar in her cup. Drinking coffee from a china cup made her feel like a real adult.

Owen watched from behind a tree. She saw him there, peeking out at the party. Owen was fourteen.

The next morning when Emily went outside, Owen jumped down from a tree, where he had been waiting. He walked on his hands across the yard for her, then fell in a heap. Emily laughed at the boy. Owen didn't like that.

"Come on," he said. "You don't know anyone else who can do that." He sprang to the porch and stood before her.

"I'm sorry," Emily said. "I shouldn't have laughed. You make a very fine monkey, sir." She wondered if he noticed her eyes were the color of emeralds.

"Where's your watch?"

"It's not a watch, Owen. It's a locket. Ladies don't wear watches."

Owen wasn't through. He stood on his hands again, his feet against the house, then walked upside down for two steps before crumbling into a ball on the porch.

"I have something for you," he said, dusting himself off.

"What is it?" Emily wanted to know.

Owen shrugged.

"Maybe you won't like it."

"Maybe I won't." It was probably some bit of something he carried in that old snuff tin he always had in his pocket.

"You can't tell."

"What is it, Owen?"

"You have to promise you won't tell anyone. You have to swear it and spit in your hand. And if you tell, your eyes will fall out and your feet will catch fire."

What he had for Emily was in the woods, he said. Emily didn't mind. She had played in the woods around the house her whole life. She knew the secret places better than Owen did. Owen picked up a stick at the edge of the trees. Emily followed him on a trail she knew by heart.

"If it's the spring, I've already seen it," Emily said.

"Further," Owen said.

Eventually, deep into the woods where the oldest trees stood, Owen stopped.

"Where is it?"

"You have to kiss me first," he said.

"I will not."

"But you must."

He stood still in front of her. There was a bit of dirt on his cheek. She couldn't kiss him there. Emily stepped forward and looked at his face for a clean spot.

"Close your eyes," Emily said.

Owen closed his eyes to slits, trying to keep one of them open just a little bit. Emily leaned toward him on her toes and lightly touched a clean place on his cheek with her lips, then quickly pulled her face away. It wasn't really a kiss at all. But Owen wouldn't know the difference.

Owen stumbled backwards. He was all grins.

"Over here," he said.

He showed her the tree. It was an ancient oak that had been split by lightning and hollowed by age. Emily had already seen it. She knew the way to the tree and back. She'd been this far into the woods many times. The opening in the tree was slim and narrow, beginning about three feet off the ground and going up. It was just wide enough that you could climb inside and hide if you had to.

"Why, Owen, you can't give me a tree that belongs to my daddy."

"It's not the tree," he said. "Look inside."

Cradled in the leaves at the bottom of the hollow was a treat indeed. It was a fuzzy puppy. The puppy looked up at Emily when she stuck her head inside.

"Owen!" Emily exclaimed. "Is he yours? Did you put him here?"

She wanted to reach in the hollow tree and pick up the puppy. She wanted to take him home and find a place in one of her father's barns for him. He was just a ball of fur. He needed milk.

"He's a wolf," Owen said proudly.

"He's a puppy," Emily said, not believing him. "He's all alone."

"Bet he's worth a silver dollar at the store," Owen said.

"Owen, you can't sell him. He's my birthday present. You already said. How did he get inside the tree? You put him there, I know you did."

"His mother hid him in the tree. Then she ran off. They shot her the other day down by Underman's Creek. First wolf anyone's seen around here in ten years, they said. Been killing sheep. Don't you hear any news at your house?"

Emily looked inside the tree. He was just a puppy.

"How come he doesn't make any noise?"

"Wolf puppies don't. They make noise, an owl will get them," Owen said with authority.

"Give me your shirt to put him in," Emily said. "I'm taking him home. He's starving to death."

"Can't. They'll kill him. They kill all the wolves. That's why there aren't any left, 'cept this one."

"Shut up, Owen. And take off your shirt."

She wrapped the small bundle of fur and feet and face in Owen's shirt and carried it against her chest on the walk home. The puppy snuggled against her. He didn't mind being carried the least bit.

The big bay colt whinnied when she walked by with

her bundle. It snorted. Emily found a wooden box in the horse barn and lined it with hay. She carefully unwrapped the puppy and gave Owen back his shirt. Emily told him to run off now.

"If you tell anyone, Owen, I'll write your name on a piece of paper and bury it in the ground. When the worms eat that piece of paper, you'll get holes in your stomach and die."

Owen knew it was true. He wasn't going to tell anyone, anyway. All he'd wanted was a kiss. And later, she would marry him, of course.

Emily brought milk and a pinch of meat from the house. The fuzzy puppy had a little red tongue and a tiny tail. His eyes were barely open. Emily figured he was as young as a puppy could be and still live without his mother. He went to sleep after he lapped the milk. She hid the puppy box at the back of the barn and placed a flour sack over the box.

She couldn't stay away. When Emily returned, she decided it was okay to pick the puppy up in her hands. She held him for a while. He was warm. The fuzzy puppy stood upon his legs when she put him back in the box. She held her finger to his mouth, and he licked her once, then nibbled at the tip of her finger.

Emily was surprised to discover that the puppy had teeth. They were sharp. She let him chew her finger. Then the puppy bit her too hard. Not on purpose. But it hurt like a needle. Emily drew her hand back. There was a spot of bright red blood on her finger.

She ran into the house and, without saying a word to

anyone, found her sewing scissors. Emily dashed back to the barn. She was in such a hurry that she frightened the horses. They stamped around inside their stalls as if something were expected of them. Emily rushed to the cool, dark corner of the barn and lifted the flour sack. She snipped a few hairs from the puppy's tail and placed them on her finger. It wasn't bad, really. The puppy was too young to have rabies. If he was sick, he wouldn't be alive at all, she reasoned. Then she had another thought and cut more hair from the puppy's back, until she had enough to make a lock of it.

***

"Something's wrong with the horses," her father said at supper. "They're acting up."

"Maybe a blacksnake is in the hay again," Emily's mother said. Horses can smell snakes.

Before Emily went to bed, she got out her birthday locket. The puppy hair was too short to braid, and it wouldn't form a proper curl. She rolled the clipped hair into a thick, short strand with her fingers and placed it inside the silver locket. She warmed the locket in her hand before putting it around her neck.

When the puppy got older, they would see he wasn't a wolf, she figured. In a week or two, by the end of August, she'd show her parents. They'd let her keep him, and she would come up with a proper name for her pet. Emily took the locket off. If she wore it to bed, the chain would tangle.

She slept with the window open so she could smell the perfume of the moonflower opening up. Planted on a small trellis, which it climbed off as much as on, the moonflower opened its large, white trumpet flowers at night, releasing a heavy perfume that was gone by morning. The flowers closed up and died in the morning sun. They did not last the day.

Emily fell fast asleep. A known narcotic, moonflower is one of the most strongly scented flowers, and one of the most poisonous of all plants. Its large, white blossoms are the size of handkerchiefs and can be seen plainly at night. Ingesting even the smallest portion of any part of the plant results in an hallucinogenic coma that lasts for days. A larger portion is fatal. The nocturnal perfume of a moonflower is said to induce dreams.

Moonflower was a popular plant throughout the Victorian period. It was grown under bedroom windows, as were Emily's mother's plants, to provide a heavenly scent on the summer breeze when the windows were open at bedtime. Moonflower blooms late in the season, when August nights are at their warmest.

Emily dreamed she was running through the woods in her nightclothes. When she came out the other side, she was standing in a pasture with her hands covered in blood. It was not the sort of dream she was used to. There was something heavy in her mouth. She ran back into the woods, to the hollow tree, and stuck her head inside. Her puppy waited. It was dark as pitch in the hollow of the oak tree, but she could see clearly. Emily dreamed her own face was covered with fur.

The bay colt bolted when Emily came into the barn the next morning, surprising her. She hurried to the puppy with milk she'd hidden in her skirt. She fed him a small amount of meat and cleaned his box.

Two weeks later, the fuzzy puppy was fat and happy. His legs had grown. He made puppy squeaks whenever she picked him up.

Emily's finger was entirely healed.

The puppy loved Emily now. And he liked meat. Instead of drinking the milk first, he gulped down the raw meat in a single mouthful. He lapped up the milk almost reluctantly.

One morning, Emily nearly screamed when she approached the puppy box. Someone had brought food to the puppy during the night. Parts of a sheep's internal organs were at the edge of the box. Blood was smeared everywhere. It smelled awful. One of the farm's hounds must have found the puppy and brought him food. Dogs, she bet, could hear the tiny sounds the puppy made.

Emily quickly cleaned up and found a larger box. She could barely carry it up the steps to the loft.

"You cannot come in the barn with me," Emily informed Owen when he showed up to see whether Emily's birthday gift was thriving.

"Why not? I've done it before."

"Mother might be watching from the window. It wouldn't look right."

Owen sulked.

"I'll go myself then," he finally said.

"Can't. I found a new hiding place. He's not in the barn anymore." Emily lied to protect her charge. "Besides, it won't be long until I can say he followed me home. Maybe he fell off a wagon on the road. They'll let me keep him, Owen. He's going to be my dog."

"He'll be ours, when you marry me."

"*If* I marry you," Emily said. "There'll be lots of fellows around when it's my time to wed."

Upon reaching full flower, a young woman with eyes like emeralds would have her choice of men.

"Two sheep are dead," Emily's father said.

Mrs. Burt and Emily listened with interest.

"It's the other wolf, according to Underman. He says they live in pairs. The one he shot was only half the problem. This one's smarter."

"Won't the dogs run it off?" Emily's mother asked.

"The wolf slipped by the dogs. It herded the sheep into the woods and slaughtered them there. One each night, the last two nights. It's smart enough to cut a sheep from the flock. It's doing it without making a sound. The dogs don't even know it's happened. It's killing wantonly now. It's not eating the sheep, but carrying off small pieces of them."

"Can't the wolf be trapped?"

"Maybe it can," Mr. Burt said. "And maybe it will have to be hunted by lantern light. If there was a pair, there may also be a litter somewhere. We'll have to find that, too."

Her father looked at Emily and waited. She glanced away. She might have suggested that one of Underman's hounds had turned wild on the sheep. But she decided it was best if she didn't say anything. If Owen had told her father about the puppy in the hollow tree, she'd never speak to him again. Not ever. She'd shoot him with her father's gun if he tried to come into the yard. She'd leap on his back and bite his neck until he fell to the ground. The idea of biting Owen's neck surprised her. Emily wondered why she thought of it. It wasn't anything she'd read in one of her books.

Emily wore her silver locket to bed. She knew she shouldn't, but she didn't care. It would keep the puppy safe to have his hair near her heart.

That night, she heard the puppy crying in her sleep. Thunder shook the woods. Rain slashed into Emily's bedroom through the open window.

The sudden storm woke Emily's mother. She rose from bed to check the windows and doors. She carried a lighted lamp into Emily's room. To her shock, her daughter wasn't there. Mrs. Burt closed the window. On her way to get her husband out of bed, Emily's mother heard a noise downstairs.

"Emily? Emily, is that you?"

"Yes, Mother," Emily said, having just come inside the back door.

She stood at the bottom of the stairway in her night-clothes, her hair and clothing soaking wet, her feet muddy and bare. Emily didn't carry a lamp, and her mother could barely see her daughter's figure at the foot of the stairs.

Mrs. Burt walked to the head of the stairway. She held the lamp before her. She stepped down the first two risers.

"For heaven's sake, child, where have you been?"

"I went to the barn. The door was banging in the storm, and I was afraid the horses would run outside. They were making a dreadful noise."

Emily had little trouble seeing in the darkness.

"My feet are dirty, Mother. Let me wash up in the kitchen and find a towel for my hair. I'll lock the door, then come back to bed."

All the windows were closed on the first floor. They always were at night.

"Don't be long," Mrs. Burt told her daughter. "And put on something dry before you go to bed."

The next morning, Owen sat in a chair in the Burts' parlor. When he rose to leave, Mr. Burt called his daughter in from the backyard. Owen wore socks and shoes. His hair was combed. Something dire was happening, Emily was sure. The youth nodded to Emily on his way out the door.

"Emily, sit down," her father said.

"Yes, sir."

"Another sheep was killed last night, just before the storm struck."

"Yes, Father."

"You understand the seriousness of what's happening, don't you? Our livelihood is at stake."

Emily folded her hands in her lap. She looked at her portrait on the wall, then glanced quickly away. She'd been a baby then. Now, Emily was a mother in her own right. She wasn't the same girl.

"Owen's father sent him over here. The boy had been keeping a secret, and it involves you. He says you found the wolves' den in the woods and that you made him promise not to tell."

"It was just a puppy, Father," Emily said. "A helpless puppy."

"In a hollow tree, was it?"

Emily nodded.

"Where's the puppy now?"

"I don't know," Emily lied. "It ran away. I think an owl may have eaten it, or something worse, much worse."

"Don't cry, Emily. This is not a matter for tears. Dry your eyes and take me to the tree. At once, do you hear?"

"Yes, Father."

Owen hadn't told him the puppy was in the barn. She might not have to kill him after all.

When they came to the lightning-split oak, Mr. Burt was puzzled to see his daughter's footprints in the drying mud. Emily tried to explain. She was there this morning, she said, to see if the puppy had come back. She thought the storm might have frightened him.

"In your bare feet?"

"I climbed inside the tree," Emily said. "I didn't want to ruin my shoes. I set them on the rock over there." She pointed to an appropriate place.

Her father checked the entire area for wolf tracks. He found none.

That night, Emily rose from bed without thinking about what she was doing. An inner urge, an instinct, brought her to the window. She looked outside. The moon was full. She could see perfectly. A mouse ran between the flower beds. Moonflowers had opened in the darkness. She drank in the perfume and, without lighting a lamp, went downstairs. Barefoot, she ran to Owen's house. It wasn't far.

Emily circled his family's house in her nightclothes, thinking to tap at his window to see if she could wake him. The dog tied to the back porch began to bark and wouldn't stop. She had to leave. The hunting hounds, in wire pens behind the smokehouse, would start yodeling soon. *Stupid dogs!*

She dashed from the yard. Her hair fell into her eyes as she trotted through the darkness. It always did when she was out at night. It didn't trouble her. It felt good to Emily to have her hair in her face, to feel her pulse pounding with every step. It felt right. A sharp pebble cut her foot. She didn't notice it.

⚜

Men armed with guns, Mr. Burt and fourteen-year-old Owen among them, hid in the shadows of the trees at the edge of the sheep pasture. All but the two best herding dogs had been penned. The two dogs were sent to the far side of the pasture, where they sat their normal vigil. The wolf, the men figured, would avoid the dogs, would approach the sheep from the cover of trees. No lantern was lit. No words were spoken.

The wolf would smell them, of course. But living so close to their homes, perhaps it had become accustomed to the scent and would not allow it to deter a raid on the helpless sheep.

They didn't see the raider approach. They didn't hear a thing. But Owen, at the farthest post, believed he saw a sheep being moved in the moonlight. One sheep at the edge of the herd looked as if it were rolling on the ground. It moved in short, jerking motions, then lay still. In a moment, squinting his eyes as hard as he could, Owen saw what he'd been waiting for.

He moved quietly among the trees, carrying his black-powder gun upright, moving nearer to the wolf's apparent angle of escape.

It moved quickly, so quickly that he lost sight of it. Owen stepped out of the trees. There it was! Taller than he had expected. A trick of the moonlight made the hunched, running animal appear almost pure white.

He counted one second. He shouldered his gun. He counted two seconds. He led the moving beast, his aim now in line with the trees. He counted the third second, upon which he held his breath and fired his gun.

The sound roared through the night. The flash of powder reflected in Owen's eyes, creating a blind spot, but he thought he saw the moving figure falter. It stumbled, it seemed, then moved on and was gone. Had he missed it entirely, the animal giving pause to the noise of the gun and nothing else? Men shouted and came running toward him. Someone whistled, and the dogs left their posts to cross the pasture and join the men. Lanterns were lit. In the distance, a long, high howl was heard.

"You hit it sure," Owen's father said. "I heard it scream. Where is it, son? Which way do I look?" He could not keep the excitement from his voice.

Owen had heard only the roar of his gun. Mr. Burt and Mr. Underman carried lanterns. The dogs found the blood. The men examined the spot with their lanterns. The wolf was wounded, but it hadn't fallen.

"Unlucky shot," Mr. Burt told the boy. "I thought you had it sure."

"Best to keep the dogs out of the woods at night," Mr.

Underman advised. "We'll track it in the morning. It may be dead already, though. That looks like a lot of blood to me. If you got it in the torso or the neck, it'll be dead before the sunrise. The dogs can follow the trail in a jiffy, come morning. We'll have it before the day is out, one way or the other."

Mr. Burt walked home, the wick trimmed low on his lantern. Moonlight filled the road, and he barely needed the light. He'd found the puppy in the barn, of course. But he had left him there. Emily's father didn't know what to do with him for now. If they got the wolf tonight, perhaps he'd build a pen and see if Emily could raise the puppy to be tame. His own father had raised a baby fox once.

If the wolf weren't found tomorrow, though, he'd have to consider using the puppy for bait. A remedy would then need to be decided upon. Emily would favor neither of the choices available to him.

Mr. Burt arrived home to discover that a horrible accident had taken place.

"She must be taken to the doctor tonight," Mrs. Burt told her husband.

"No," he said flatly. "No."

They treated their daughter's arm and gave her morphine, which Mr. Burt had on supply in case of major injury to one of the farm hands. She talked nonsense. Mrs. Burt sewed closed the worst of the opening in her daughter's skin. Nothing the girl said made sense to her father. Not a single word of it.

"She has to see a doctor," Mrs. Burt insisted. "She's

only twelve, for God's sake!"

Mr. Burt said his prayers, drank Scotch whiskey, and prayed.

Late the next morning, the hunt for the wounded wolf was called off. It had made its escape, despite the blood left for the dogs to trail. The hounds found their way time and time again to a hollow tree deep in the woods, where the trail was lost. The dogs drifted then toward Mr. Burt's plantation, entering the property near the barn, where it came upon them to harass the horses stabled there. The dogs could not be made to cease their baying and were led away.

That evening, Owen knocked on the Burts' front door. He inquired of Emily's health. Emily was as fine as to be expected. Owen asked if he might be allowed to speak to her. He was told that would be impossible.

"I found this in the yard on my way to the door," Owen said, lying.

He held out his hand to Emily's mother. In his palm was cradled the silver locket with Emily's monogram engraved on the face of it. She accepted it on her daughter's behalf and thanked the boy for its safe return.

"Will you be raising the puppy, then?" Owen asked Mr. Burt.

"I may give it a try," Emily's father said. "If that wolf doesn't come back, that is."

The three of them hoped it wouldn't. Especially Owen, who knew the truth. He'd found the locket at a spot near where the wolf had been wounded the night before. He spotted it between the blood in the grass and where the wolf had entered the woods. The sunlight caught the facets engraved in the silver locket, and for a moment, it looked to Owen as if he'd found emeralds on the ground.

Emily, her parents decided, would be sent to visit her cousins in Europe as soon as she could travel. There was a doctor in Paris who was known around the world for his treatment of psychological disorders. His specialty was curing lycanthropy—the delusion of one possessed by the belief that he or she is a werewolf.

Neighbors heard the story a different way. They were told that Emily Burt had been playing with her father's pistol in the barn loft, that she had tripped coming down the wooden steps inside the barn. The gun fell from the young girl's grasp and discharged when it hit the ground, sending a pistol ball through the flesh of her arm. Gangrene had been avoided, as had other serious infection. Emily was quite well, in fact, spending time with family in Philadelphia.

Emily eventually returned home to live out her life on the Burt plantation in Talbot County, Georgia. She never married. She had a pet dog that some people said was a wolf. They didn't know its name. Although she was occasionally asked, Emily never offered an opinion on the finer qualities of the city of Philadelphia.

She died in 1911 and was buried in a family cemetery along Jeff Hendrix Road in Belleview, Georgia. The cemetery is on a hill surrounded by four magnolia trees and a rock wall. The magnolia trees are believed to be at least 150 years old.

The Open Door

Edisto Island, South Carolina

Happiness for a dog, it has been said, is the other side of a door. Any door.

Throughout the South, the War Between the States separated thousands of young men from their homes and from their country. Wearing uniforms and carrying flags newly created for the crisis, Southern men marched into battle against a government that had once been their own. Most Confederate soldiers believed they were defending their homes and families against armed invasion. You would likely do the same.

War removes young men from their parents, their wives, and their children. It also separates them from their dogs.

Dogs put up with this as best they can. Dogs know how to wait.

John Beaujot Legare (pronounced *Legree*) was the son of a prominent rice grower on Edisto Island. The family was descended of the founders of the island community on the Atlantic coast of South Carolina. They cultivated crops of rice and indigo. By the 1790s, Edisto Islanders were known for the production of sea-island cotton, one of the finest cottons ever grown. Sea-island cotton brought great wealth to Edisto Island. Many of the elegant houses and plantations remaining today, sites listed in the National Register of Historic Places, are reminders of that affluent age.

John Legare's father died when John was yet very young. John lived with his mother in a large home at the end of a tree-lined lane. Stately oaks, their branches draped with Spanish moss, were common on the island. Neighboring uncles trained John in the management of his inherited rice plantation. John was content to learn his trade as a planter. He proved proficient and became as successful at managing the crop and the plantation as his father had been.

Soon after his father's death, John was given a puppy he named Moses. A close bond formed between the two. The dog went everywhere John did. John never left the house without Moses. When John went to church with his mother on Sunday, Moses waited outside, likely wondering what all the singing was about.

The only thing Moses liked even half as much as John was buttermilk biscuits. Moses was allowed in the kitchen in the morning. He was trained by his master to wait until

John had finished eating. Then Moses was given the leftover breakfast biscuits, sometimes with a little gravy. The dog would never eat until John was done. It was a simple rule and one that Moses understood and abided by.

"I was thinking this old place could use some children," John told his mother one morning. He was twenty now and felt like a man.

"Do you have anyone in particular in mind?"

His mother had been thinking the same thing. John had proved he could manage his affairs with competence and attention to detail. When there was work to be done, it was done. It was time he thought about raising children.

John shook his head.

"I don't know much about courting a wife, Mother. I was hoping you might be able to instruct me in the art. What did Father do to win your heart?"

"Oh, there were many things. But surely, you don't mean to court just anyone, John."

John thought about it.

"I guess she'd have to like my dog."

After breakfast, Moses was led outside. As he did every day, he trotted quickly to the front of the house, clambered on the porch, and lay by the door, waiting for John to come outside. A rabbit hopped from behind a tree and twitched its nose. Moses watched the rabbit with interest. He came alert while the rabbit was in view but would not budge from his vigil at the front door. Not until John came out.

As far as Moses was concerned, John's coming out the front door in his walking boots was the rising of the sun that started the day. They had the entire island to explore and many important functions to perform. There were frogs to catch and horses that sorely required being barked at. There were literally hundreds of smelly spots in the sand along the ocean's edge that needed digging. And you couldn't end the day, really, without putting a stick in your mouth and chasing off a sea gull.

Edisto Island was long an isolated marshland community with two churches and a single one-lane wooden bridge connecting it to the mainland. It did not, however, remain removed from our country's greatest tragedy. No community in the American South, no matter how isolated by custom or geography, was spared involvement in the War Between the States. With the firing on Fort Sumter at the mouth of Charleston Harbor on April 12, 1861, the South was engaged in war.

Almost immediately upon hearing of the action at Fort Sumter, John Legare enlisted in Company A of Johnson Hagood's First South Carolina Volunteer Infantry. He left behind a mother distraught with fear she would never see her son again. He left behind a plantation home and a mongrel dog named Moses.

Moses had been John's devoted companion for several years. John couldn't leave his house without Moses' following him, or leading him. Being with John was what the dog lived for. There was adventure and purpose in life when the dog was in John's company. There hadn't been a single day in the existence of Moses when he hadn't seen John. Until war came, that is. Until John left home without him.

Moses moped something horrible. He would barely eat

the first few weeks. He paced the property and lay around on the porch. At the end of the day, Moses would curl up outside the door of the Legare home and wait.

Moses was not in general comforted by the attention of John's mother. Mrs. Legare believed the dog felt worse about the war than she did, if that were possible. The thing about Moses was he seemed to know that a letter from John was coming. He trotted to the end of the Legares' lane at the main road first thing one morning, then waited until the messenger came with a rare letter from John.

Mrs. Legare stood on the porch, tearing the wax seal and weeping over the words from her boy soldier. He wrote of his deep devotion to God, of needing better food and better clothes. He wrote of his hope of returning soon. He wrote of his hope of war's end.

Moses lay down at her feet, his head resting between his outstretched front legs, his eyebrows twitching at the sound of Mrs. Legare's sobs. Moses would have cried, too, if he'd known how. Once she dried her tears, Mrs. Legare read parts of the letter aloud to Moses, who sat up to listen. The dog knew the words were from John. Mrs. Legare believed it was important that Moses should hear them.

"My dear mother, I beg you, do not under any circumstances allow the fair ladies of Edisto to marry during this dread conflict, for I shall soon demand the hand of the finest of them upon my return. Tell them one, I pray, and tell them all that a gallant knight will be home very soon.

"Though, dear mother, my eyes have seen what my heart cannot hold, a gallant knight I shall most surely be on the day of my return. They should settle for no man less than he during this awful time of woe. Tell them, Mother, to be brave."

Moses lifted one eyebrow and then the other as she read the words out loud.

Then Mrs. Legare made up some words for Moses, as if she were reading them from John's letter.

"Please send my gentlest regards to Moses," she said. "And give my faithful and handsome dog my share of biscuits tomorrow at breakfast."

Moses twitched his ears. It was the only time he was at all happy.

Mrs. Legare stooped to pet the dog's head, then continued her feigned reading.

"Tussle his ragged fur and tell my dog I miss him like the dickens!"

His tail wagged.

"Dear mother, if there be a flea about his ragged fur, please remove it at once for me. This be your dutiful son's only request."

Mrs. Legare rubbed Moses' back. She scratched his neck and tugged his ears. At this moment, it was as if she were somehow able to touch her son by petting his dog. Moses let her.

When she was through, Moses stood up and walked in a circle three times before lying back down on the porch with a small grunt. Then there was a long, sad sigh. Moses looked off into the distance. He looked down the tree-lined lane to the rutted road. He waited for John.

Late one day in August of the next year, Moses took to the road in front of the Legare home. He sat down in the wagon tracks and could not be made to budge. People on horseback rode around him. Moses never so much as looked at them. He sat there all night.

In the morning, Mrs. Legare walked the oak-lined lane from her house to the road.

"What is it, Moses? Is a letter coming from John today?"

She'd never known him to sit in the road the night before a letter arrived. Moses stayed there the rest of the day. No letter came.

Mrs. Legare had trouble sleeping. She believed she could hear the distant sound of guns. She left the lamps in the house lit.

The next morning, Moses was still there.

He stood on four feet upon Mrs. Legare's arrival. Moses took a biscuit from her hand, then began to walk down the dusty road. She followed him, lifting her skirts an inch or two from the ground to keep from ruining the hems. She followed Moses to the wooden bridge that connected the island to the mainland. He didn't look back to see if she was coming.

Moses stopped at the end of the bridge and looked across, whining. There was nothing to see on the other side. He would not stop staring. It was as if something important were coming and he couldn't see it yet. Dogs sometimes know when something is about to happen that neither you nor they can see.

It was a terribly hot day, and Mrs. Legare grew impatient with Moses. What if someone came by and asked her what she was doing there? What could she possible say? She was watching for John's return from the battlefields of war. She couldn't possibly say that. It wasn't brave. More likely, Mrs. Legare decided, she was merely watching her son's dog behave badly for no reason at all. In August, the mosquitoes and biting flies were out in the middle of the day, and she should be inside.

"Come on, Moses," she said. "Let's go home. Nothing's coming by way of the bridge today."

Moses whined.

"Come on, I said! We're needed home."

Eventually, Mrs. Legare convinced Moses to abandon his vigil. Moses turned without looking at her and walked home.

When John came back from war, he would come to the house. Moses stayed in the road out front.

The next day, September 1, 1862, a man was dispatched to the Legare home. He walked with slow purpose from the grocery store, saying hello to Moses as he passed by.

Moses ignored him. It was not John.

He trod the shaded lane to the Legare house. If there were birds singing in the trees, he did not notice. The man had sad news for Mrs. Legare. On August 30, two days past, Confederate private John Beaujot Legare shouldered an Enfield rifle at the Battle of Second Manassas and was felled. Her son's body would arrive on Edisto Island later that day. Moses had taken to the road at the moment John Legare began the long journey home.

Mrs. Legare covered the mirrors and put on black.

Everyone on the barrier island who could walk attended the funeral at the Presbyterian church. When the appropriate words had been said, John's casket was carried from the church. Outside, Moses barked at the pallbearers carrying his fallen master away. No one told him to stop it. People of the rural South understand the bond between a dog and a man.

John Legare's body was entombed in the family mausoleum on the grounds of the church near the main road on Edisto Island, where he would lay in perpetual rest alongside the casket of his sister Julia, who had succumbed to fever in 1852.

While close friends offered Mrs. Legare their condolences, Moses trotted inside the mausoleum to be with John's body. He could not be made to leave his master's side. Moses proved time and time again, by baring his teeth and growling with sudden ferocity, that he was determined to stay. Mrs. Legare insisted the heavy marble door of the mausoleum be left open until the dog decided on his own accord to end his mourning.

Food and water were brought to the mausoleum and placed inside. Moses refused to eat. He never raised his head again, it is said. Mrs. Legare brought buttermilk biscuits to the mausoleum and tried to feed him by hand. Moses wouldn't take a bite. Over the course of the next several days, Moses slowly passed away.

Mrs. Legare understood. She grieved the loss of her son for the rest of her life and never again experienced a healthy appetite.

The mausoleum was sealed.

Mrs. Legare had Moses carried home and buried in the back garden. She placed the letters John had written her into the grave with Moses. She believed he needed them. Mrs. Legare marked the location with a piece of slate.

What Moses needed most was to be with John. In death, it seems he accomplished just that.

A few days later, it was noticed that the marble door of the mausoleum had come open. It was closed again. A few days after that, it was found open once more. Mrs. Legare was told of the problem. Iron chains were then used to secure the mausoleum door.

They were to no avail. The chains were found broken, the heavy door pushed in from the outside.

It was Moses.

Separated for so long from his master in life, the faithful dog stubbornly refused to be separated from his master in the afterlife. They should have been buried together, Mrs. Legare believed. She asked the elders of the church to leave the door as it was, to leave it open. Like dogs and little boys, ghosts require companionship, too.

Even though Moses was a ghost, he wanted nothing more than to be at his master's side each morning. If John couldn't open the mausoleum door and come outside, Moses would open it for him. He'd waited long enough for John to come home.

The Presbyterian church on Edisto Island can be visited today.

The sanctuary, erected in 1830, was designed by Charleston architect James Curtis. But the church is much older. It was founded in 1685. The cemetery that surrounds three sides of the church dates to the early 1700s. Shaded by stately moss-hung oaks, the graveyard is hauntingly beautiful. It is also haunted.

After Mrs. Legare died, the mausoleum became the worry of the church. Over the years, a variety of methods were used to seal the marble structure, but somehow Moses always managed to get inside. In the late 1960s, the door was attached in such a way that it could be opened only by using heavy equipment. Moses was well over a hundred years old by then (more like four hundred, in ghost-dog years). Still, he got in. The door was soon found broken in three pieces and fallen to the ground. If it were a battle of wills, Moses won. The marble door was finally secured face-down with concrete to the mausoleum floor, a piece of the original chain still attached. The vault remains open to this day. Nothing man can do will keep Moses away.

The bridge to Edisto Island, now part of Highway 174, has been vastly improved. A portion of the Atlantic beachfront is now a state park. It remains one of the few unspoiled beach areas on the East Coast. Edisto is a quiet, family island. Private homes are put on tour once a year by the Edisto Island Historic Preservation Society.

Permanent residents require little formality. The people who live on the island place a premium on preserving nature and history. They know all about the open door of the Legare mausoleum and will gladly point the way to the Presbyterian cemetery. Occasionally savaged by the howling rage of hurricanes, islanders don't fret the small stuff and have no difficulty tolerating a door left open for a fellow islander's devoted pet. Even if the dog's been dead for 140 some odd years now.

Vestiges of our country's war with itself exist both north and south of the Mason-Dixon line. It is a grim fact of our nation's history that 660,000 men perished in the War Between the States. As many as 500,000 American dogs were left without their masters. Moses was not one of them.

Trick or Treat

Nashville, Tennessee

Mrs. Hammond Singleton was crazy, and so was her dog. Every kid in the neighborhood knew it. Her front yard in the Belmont Hillsboro area south of Vanderbilt University was entirely planted in clover instead of grass. She wore a bonnet whenever she went outside. An eleven-year-old in 1962 needed no more evidence than this to be convinced that the old lady was certifiably insane.

Mostly, though, Cindy Linn's grandmother went bonkers on Halloween. She handed out apples to children who came to her door for treats. Not candied apples. Just apples. And that was only the beginning.

Mrs. Hammond Singleton kept a sack of acorns by the door, and every pirate, ballerina, fairy princess, and baseball player who came to her porch on Halloween had to reach into the sack and pull out an acorn and show it to her. Cindy's grandmother would read each child's fortune by looking closely at an acorn, upon which she could see a face, she said, but only on Halloween. Cindy's grandmother held a lighted candle in one hand, by which to study the acorn in her other hand. She recited a poem while squinting at each one: "On All Hallow's Eve,/When the hour is very late,/Find an acorn in the garden./Upon it read your fate."

"She's nuts," Cindy complained to her mother. "And so's Preston. He follows us to every house. He's always bumping into us. It isn't fair."

Preston was Mrs. Hammond Singleton's Boxer. The dog had the run of the neighborhood. He liked Halloween more than Cindy's grandmother did.

Cindy was a beatnik this year. She wore a black beret, black tights, and one of her father's sweatshirts that came to her knees. She tied a red scarf around her neck and was allowed to wear her mother's lipstick. She didn't know for certain if beatniks wore lipstick. But Halloween was the only time Cindy was allowed to wear it, and she certainly wasn't going to pass up the opportunity to wear lipstick on a night when she might see Ernie Rousch from across the street.

Ernie was almost thirteen.

"Having a dog behind me all night doesn't go with my costume, Mom."

Preston knew all the stops. He knew most of the kids in the neighborhood, too. His daily routine, as soon as Mrs. Hammond Singleton let him out of the house, was to secure the entire area. He made a series of rounds each day, six blocks in one direction, six in another, four this way, six that, and back.

Preston was a solitary inspector. He made sure every mailbox was in place. He checked the trees and bushes to see if they were growing as they should. He counted the bicycles, tricycles, and water sprinklers left on the lawns. He saw that the right cars were home and that the right cars were gone. He verified that the rolled newspapers that wouldn't be picked up until the end of day were where they should be.

Dogs in fenced backyards along his route barked as Preston came by. They said hello or alerted him that small pieces of neighborhood were already ably guarded. Preston took down the information as a mental note but never barked back. He had work to do. He was too busy to play.

At one house, he was given a dog biscuit. The young housewife was there every day. If she wasn't, the dog biscuit was sitting on her concrete step as a signal to Preston that everything was okay. In front of another home, a large tabby cat waited in the middle of the sidewalk. When Preston came by, the cat hopped up and followed him to the end of the block, keeping a respectful distance.

Preston possessed a deep sense of community responsibility. And he dearly loved Halloween. It was the one night of the year when people went out to learn his job. He was pleased to accompany them, even if the children were noisy and slow to learn. They couldn't go sixteen steps without eating something.

When children stopped to tie a shoe or repair the rubber band on a mask, Preston hurried back to check on them. He'd even push them a little from the side if they took too long. Then it was important that he catch up to the front again. He would brush by others on the sidewalk to get to the place where he'd left off.

Preston followed Cindy and her friends every Halloween, bumping them when they went too slow, cutting them off if they tried to overlook a house. He'd hurry to the front door to show them where they were going. Then he'd fall back, bumping them once again, and wait on the sidewalk until they had learned the people who lived there and counted the things in the yard.

It was a marvelous job, really. And no dog was better prepared for Halloween duty than Preston. On top of which, being a white-chested, light tan Boxer with black markings, including the traditional black around both eyes, he already had a mask.

Cindy was instructed that she was not only going to her grandmother's house this Halloween, she was going there first.

"She's looking for you, and you aren't going to make her wait, young lady."

"There's bees in her yard," Cindy complained, using up her last excuse.

"Not at night," her mother said. "And they won't bother you anyway, if you stay on the sidewalk."

When she was thirteen, she wasn't doing this anymore, Cindy decided.

She hiked all the way to her grandmother's house with Brenda and Julie, her two best friends.

"She'll ask you to sing," Cindy warned them.

But Brenda and Julie had been to Mrs. Hammond Singleton's before on Halloween. They knew the routine. If you didn't sing, you had to dance to get a treat. If you didn't want to dance, you could get your treat by standing on one foot with your eyes closed.

Brenda and Julie stood behind Cindy when the door opened.

"Hi, Grandma. It's me," Cindy said.

Mrs. Hammond Singleton held the candle out in front of her as if she couldn't believe her eyes.

"Cindy?" she asked. "Are you sure it's you? I thought it was a movie star."

Preston waited inside the door while the three girls chose acorns and had their fortunes told. Cindy would marry a man with a mustache and have eight children, four boys and four girls. Brenda would marry a sailor and have four children, all girls, who would marry sailors when they grew up. Julie would marry a preacher and live in a foreign country. India, Mrs. Hammond Singleton thought it would be, but she wasn't sure it might not be China or Pakistan. They stood on one foot with their eyes closed while Cindy's grand-mother dropped an apple in each of their sacks.

"Thank you, Grandma," Cindy said.

"Don't go by the church tonight," Mrs. Hammond Singleton advised the girls. "Circle back the other way. The ghost doubles of those who are doomed to die during the coming year parade through the churchyard on Halloween."

"Okay," Cindy said. "We won't."

Preston trotted out the door as Cindy and her friends walked back to the street, giggling. The fortunes weren't real ones. They were going to marry Elvis Presley, if they married anyone. Or maybe Ernie Rousch. He was almost thirteen and could probably grow a mustache if he wanted to.

Preston went to work counting houses. He took note of trick-or-treaters coming from the other direction. He crossed the street to take inventory, double-checking on the littlest children. Preston liked the littlest ones the best. They worked hard at it, with serious intent, and didn't lollygag like the older kids. Once the newcomers were accounted for, Preston ran to catch up to Cindy and her friends.

Preston bumped into Cindy to let her know he was there.

"Cut it out," she said.

They were getting close to Ernie's house. That summer, Cindy had written her and Ernie's initials in chalk on the sidewalk in front of his house. It was the bravest thing she'd ever done. If he were there tonight, he would see her in lipstick.

Ernie wasn't home, but the girls could peer into the living room through the front window. They saw the couch where Ernie sat when he was home.

"Ask to use the bathroom," Julie said.

"No!" Cindy squealed. "You ask."

When they reached the next block, the girls talked about going back to Ernie's house. He might be home by then.

In the middle of the block, a second-grader had dropped his sack of candy in the street. His older brother was already at the door of the next house. The little guy tried to pick up every piece of candy on the pavement. His Halloween mask made it a difficult task. But he wasn't leaving any. The seven-year-old had worked hard for his treats.

Preston bumped Cindy again. This time, he was trying to get around her to the street. He was the only one who heard the car coming.

Cindy spun around to watch him. She'd never seen Preston run so fast.

Preston rushed with his head low and smacked hard into the little boy, who was bent over on his hands and knees. The Boxer hit the second-grader in the chest and pushed hard until his head was under the boy's stomach. The sack hastily refilled with candy went flying. So did the little boy. He landed on his bottom six or seven feet from where he'd been when Preston made contact. It hurt.

The car hit Preston squarely. It squealed its brakes. The thud was loud and certain. Cindy saw it all. She screamed.

Parents separated themselves from the trick-or-treating children and ran to the street. Several had flashlights. The driver was a college student. He was quick to open the door. The little boy wailed.

"I didn't hit the kid," the driver said.

The seven-year-old was swept up by one of the adults.

"He's okay," the man holding him said. "Just sacred. You're okay, aren't you, cowboy?"

"I didn't hit the kid," the driver said again. "I hit the dog."

Cindy ran to the front of the car, looking for Preston. He hadn't made a sound. He was surely dead or badly injured and about to die. She was afraid to find him, to see him crushed, but she had to. She looked to the front of the car, then to the left and to the right. He wasn't anywhere.

"He must have run off," someone said. "Dogs do that sometimes when they get hit. He's probably okay, then. He probably went home."

Cindy was crying. It was a horrible Halloween.

"He saved the little kid's life," Brenda said.

"Everyone saw him do it," Julie added. "We all did."

Cindy hurried home to tell her parents that Preston had been hit by a car. They'd have to look for him. Brenda and Julie came inside with her. They would help look. Brenda could call her father, and they could use his car.

"That won't be necessary," Cindy's mother said. "Are you sure it was Preston, dear?"

"Yes," Cindy said. "He came with us from Grandma's house. He was with us the whole time, like always. This little boy was in the street, and Preston ran ninety miles an hour and knocked him out of the way, and then the car hit him. It hit him real hard, Mom. Everyone heard it."

"You're sure it was Preston? You all saw him?"

The three girls nodded.

"Maybe he's back at Grandma's house. Can you tell her, Mom? Please. I just can't."

"I thought she might have told you, dear," Cindy's mother said. "I imagine she didn't want to ruin your Halloween. Preston had cancer. He died at the vet's yesterday."

Almost fifty years later, there are still trick-or-treaters in the Belmont Hillsboro neighborhood of Nashville who get bumped by a dog if they go too slowly from house to house or stand too long in the middle of the street. An old woman who was a young housewife in 1962 leaves a dog biscuit on the concrete step in front of her house once a year. On Halloween.

The old woman makes the children sing or dance for her, or at least stand on one foot with their eyes closed, before she gives them a treat. She says she learned to do this from an old widow named Mrs. Hamilton Singleton, who immigrated to this country from York, England, and who was as crazy as bees in clover. And so was her dog, Preston.

Jameson's Bell

Mobile, Alabama

Home to the oldest Mardi Gras celebration in America, the area of Mobile, Alabama, was founded as Fort Louis by the French in 1702. It was occupied by the British from 1763 to 1780 and by the Spanish from 1780 to 1813. During the War of 1812, the port was captured by United States forces under General James Wilkinson. Andrew Jackson established his headquarters here and successfully defended Mobile throughout the war. The city of Mobile was incorporated in 1819.

The occupation of Mobile by outside entities did not end with the War of 1812. Since before written history, Mobile has been with some regularity raided and occupied by devastating floods and hurricanes.

Hurricanes overtake the Gulf coast at will, coming ashore where they choose, staying as long as they like. In October 1893, two thousand people were killed when a hurricane slammed into southeastern Louisiana and southern Alabama. The ports of the American South are particularly vulnerable to the flooding that accompanies tropical storms and hurricanes. Mobile is no exception.

So it was in 1850 that locals advised against Captain Hugh Barlow's decision to build his home so close to the water on the old Bay Front Road in Mobile. Surely, his house would be lost to flood, he was told. Captain Barlow was undeterred. He knew a thing or two about water.

The retired sea captain wanted to be as close to the tide as possible. Salt water was in his blood. The rising and falling tides were his clock, his heartbeat, his dance step.

Being bound to land was difficult enough. He didn't understand how people walked on it with even a bit of grace to their step. His stride took into account that the surface beneath his feet was subject to the steady roll of waves. That's the way a man walked, with the pitch of things. On land, the earth hardly pitched at all.

Being even a foot closer to the sea was important to Captain Barlow. And he knew how to beat the floods. He had his house on the sea side of Bay Front Road built like a ship. It was erected on short pylons to begin with. The floors were made of teakwood and undercoated with tar. A large room for dancing was central to the house. The first-floor windows did not reach low on the walls, as was common in 1850. Instead, they began at waist level, the height of a ship's railing.

Captain Barlow was possessed of three passions in his life—the sea, ballroom dancing, and his dog, Jameson. Barlow named the black-and-white Spaniel after an old shipmate who was now deceased.

Dogs in the South in this period of American history were rarely kept indoors. Captain Barlow built his dog's house on the same design as his own. It became something of a fancy. Also on pylons, the doghouse had steps leading to the door. Teak was used for the floor and walls. The boards were sealed with tar. A small belfry was added to the top, upon which was mounted a weather vane. In the doghouse belfry, Captain Barlow installed the brass ship's bell he had received upon retirement. It was engraved with his name. A piece of rope dangled from the bell into the doghouse. Jameson could tug on the rope and ring the bell at will, but he rarely did. Jameson liked watching the birds in the yard, and the bell's ringing scared the birds away.

Captain Barlow had been a clever dancer the whole of his adult life. It was said he could dance the quadrilles on a ship's deck during a hurricane. He knew dances from around the world. His favorites were the waltzes.

Time, though, had taken its toll on Captain Barlow. His knees were knotted in pain in old age. He could not walk far when the pain was at its worst. Sometimes, he could barely walk at all.

Captain Barlow installed a cable from the top of the doghouse tower to a brass cleat above the back door of his house. Jameson's leash was tied in a small loop around the cable, allowing the dog to exercise in the yard and to come upon the back porch when Captain Barlow desired his company.

In 1851, the captain's only daughter, Ruth Barlow, wed Robert Ester Francis, and the couple moved into Captain Barlow's new home. The bride was a lively dancer, having learned any number of reels and polkas from her father. A grand ball was held in the house in celebration of her marriage. The first dance was to be a waltz reserved for the bride and her father.

Captain Barlow was heartbroken when, despite his desire, he could not manage to dance that night. While the orchestra played beautifully, Ruth walked slowly around the floor in her satin gown, her aged and crippled father on her arm. The pain in Barlow's legs was nearly unbearable. In his heart, he waltzed. Through her tears, his daughter accompanied him. They managed but one circuit around the room before the pain forced Captain Barlow to take a chair.

Captain Barlow's house was a splendid place. And although the grand room of the house had been constructed for the purpose, no more dances were held there in the captain's lifetime.

Ruth assisted her father in accomplishing his daily routine when the pain in his legs was at its height. Robert Francis enjoyed the older man's endless stories of life at sea.

Some people believe that human bones act as a barometer. If so, the air pressure changed dramatically on August 22, 1852.

Captain Barlow could not get out of bed. The pain in his legs would not allow him to stand. Ruth prepared a daybed on the back porch, and Robert carried the old man there so he could visit his dog.

A constable came to the door late in the day and informed the household that the town was being evacuated. Ships had been driven from the high sea into Mobile Bay by an approaching storm. Word from sailors returning from the sea was the only warning people had of hurricanes in those days. When someone saw a storm, they knew it was there.

High winds blew inland.

They must leave now, the constable said.

Captain Barlow refused. His house, he told his daughter and his son-in-law, would survive a little flooding, a few high waves.

The next morning, the ship's bell in the doghouse started ringing and wouldn't stop. Jameson wouldn't go near the doghouse. The Spaniel kept to the back porch, the persistent wind lifting his long ears, feathering the fur along his back.

It was nearly as dark as night. Storm clouds blocked the sun. Soon, torrents of rain slashed the windows and hammered the roof of Captain Barlow's teak-floored house. Waves rose from the sea and came ashore. In minutes, the storm, which has become known to history as the Great Hurricane of 1852, swept into the bay to occupy Mobile for as long as it cared to. Captain Barlow's house was washed away in the flood. It was only one of the many

changes the hurricane made of the landscape during its ravaging occupation.

⁂

In September 1979, the schooner *Lady's Day* barely made a wake as it sliced through the rolling water of the Intracoastal Waterway north of Dauphin Island, which guards the southeastern entry to Mobile Bay. The sailboat was running on its engines because it was night and the sea had begun to surge.

The *Lady's Day* was coming in from the Gulf of Mexico to dock at Mon Louis. Six people were aboard, three men and three women. They had been on the water for two days. Gordon Weems was at the helm. His son Eddie stood at the bow, watching for lights. He believed he heard a ship's bell. Straining to see, he spotted the fore corner of a small sea vessel. It might have been an overturned boat. It had no lights.

"Craft ahead!" he yelled back to his father. "Two points off bow."

Gordon cut the engine to idle and waited for instructions.

"What is it?" he shouted. He couldn't see a thing.

Eddie was intent on bringing the small craft or bit of wreckage into focus. He thought he heard a dog barking. He turned on the fore spotlight and checked the water from left to right. And there it was.

"Doghouse with a bell!" he called to his father. "We're clear on course one degree starboard!"

"One degree starboard," Gordon confirmed, and adjusted the wheel. "What did you say?"

By then, his father could see it. A doghouse was drifting to the port side. They'd miss it entirely. The doghouse was a fancy one with a bell tower and a weather vane. It rode the sea like a boat, its bell ringing as the doghouse pitched on the sea.

You see every kind of thing floating in the water off populated coastlines. But neither man had seen a doghouse before. The four others were below. In their amazement to see a doghouse floating by, neither Gordon nor Eddie called them to the deck.

Even more amazing, the doghouse had a dog. It stood in the door of its dwelling and barked at the *Lady's Day*. It looked like a Cocker Spaniel to Eddie. It was black and white and had wide, long ears hanging to either side of its face.

"Attempt a rescue!" Eddie shouted. "Hold steady. I'll throw a line."

In the sudden turn and surge of the *Lady's Day*, the light Eddie held went astray. It didn't matter anyway. When he looked up, he saw something entirely new. A large, two-story house was directly in front of them. There were people on the porch waving a lantern. He should have seen the lantern earlier, if it had been there. The house appeared as if it had been formed from air at the moment Eddie was looking at it.

Gordon saw it, too. He barely had time to alert Eddie as he spun the wheel hard to starboard and pushed the engine out of idle.

"Hold fast!" he yelled to his son. "Coming around!"

Eddie knew what *hold fast* meant. He dropped to the deck on his belly. They were seconds from collision with a house at sea.

But they didn't hit the house. The man on the porch, the one with the lantern, was shouting at Eddie. They were only a few feet away. Then the house disappeared. It vanished into thin air. Eddie thought he could still hear the ship's bell ringing, but it might have been a trick of memory. He wasn't sure.

Gordon took a moment to get his bearings as Eddie came back to the helm in a careful hurry.

"Did you see it?" he asked his father in a flush of excitement. "Did you see the house? I thought we were coming aground."

Gordon Weems wasn't ready to say what he'd seen. It had looked to him as if the doghouse was towing the big house on a long line. Then they had both disappeared.

"Did you hear what he was saying, the man on the porch?"

Gordon shook his head. He wondered if it might be possible for two men to have the same dream at the same time and be fully awake. He couldn't for the life of him have imagined a doghouse with a weather vane and a ship's bell.

" 'Hurricane,' " Eddie told his father. "That's what the man shouted. Did you hear him?"

"Best get to dock," Gordon said.

A storm was expected in the area, but not for a few days. They weren't even sure at the weather station if it was coming that way.

Eddie told the others on board and was anxious to talk to the dock captain at Mon Louis. The old man wore a navy-blue captain's hat. It had an emblem of an anchor embroidered in gold thread above the bill. Tattoos ran up the weathered skin of both forearms. The old man tugged his white beard as Eddie quickly told him what they'd seen. Gordon left the two of them standing on the dock.

" 'Hurricane,' he said, did he?"

"Have you ever heard of such a thing?" Eddie wanted to know. "A barking dog and a house. Has anyone else seen it?"

"Plenty have," the old man informed him. "A hurricane is coming for sure. You can bet on that, young man. Sailors saw that dog in August 1950, and in 1932 and 1926 before that. I heard it said that sailors on the bay had warning in 1906, and even way back in '93. It was that doghouse every time. And the house right behind it. A hurricane is coming sure."

"It's a ghost ship that looks like a house?" Eddie asked.

"No, it's a house sure enough. Captain Barlow built it to live in. And that's his doghouse, too. He built them both to float in case of a flood. Haven't you heard it told before?"

Eddie hadn't. They turned to walk to the dock house.

"Aye," the old man said, "when that dog takes to ringing the bell, a big one's coming for sure. Won't be any sailing out of my dock for the rest of the week."

Father and son rode home together in Eddie's Jeep. The others took the van. Gordon was reluctant to talk about what they'd seen, but slowly he came around. Eddie refused to speak of anything else.

"You think it's true?" Eddie asked his father.

"We should have seen the light sooner," Gordon said.

"The lantern? I don't think it was there, Dad. I think it appeared when the house did. And that old man on the porch. I could hear him plain as day."

"He was sure waving that lantern, wasn't he?"

"You know what it looked like to me, Dad? It looked like he was dancing."

Gordon had thought the same thing. The old salt in the white beard and captain's hat was dancing across that front porch to beat the band. He clogged and reeled, dipped and spun, swinging the lantern high and low.

"It was something, all right," Gordon said.

Three days later, on September 12, Hurricane Frederick occupied Mobile Bay. The city suffered an incredibly destructive storm. The hurricane damaged three out of every four buildings in Mobile. Monetary losses exceeded $2.2 billion, according to the United States Army Corps of Engineers. The orderly evacuation of more than a hundred thousand residents kept the loss of life to one person.

Captain Hugh Barlow likes to think he helped, even if Jameson's bell was heard by only a few.

The Missing Tree

Sewell's Woods, Georgia

There is more music in a good Coonhound than there is on the radio.

"Of course, that's when they're hunting," Dave Perkins told the young man who had come to look over a new litter. "You come back in two weeks, and we'll see if one of these pups likes you."

The young man wanted to meet the father of the pups.

Dave walked him to the front porch. Basie was asleep on the porch swing. Coonhounds always look bigger than they actually are because they are highly skilled at spreading out when they lie down. A good black-and-tan will take up a whole couch.

"Is he dead?"

"Saving his energy," Dave told the young man. "When he's not hunting, he gets his rest in."

"What else does he do besides sleep?"

"Sometimes, he sprawls."

The young man nodded knowingly.

"Other times, he dawdles."

"Are their ears supposed to be that big?"

Basie looked like he was wearing a short-furred towel over his head.

"You wouldn't want a Coonhound whose ears didn't reach his nose," Dave said. "The other hounds would make fun of him when he ran."

Dave's two oldest dogs, Basie and Bert, were exceptional examples of Coonhounds. They hunted possum mostly. As with other Coonhounds, their job ended when a possum was treed and the sound dog called the hunter to the location.

Coonhounds usually hunt in a group, rushing after smells through the night woods. One dog among the others becomes the sound hound once a prey is treed. The others might whine a little and toss in a coo now and then, but they only serve vocally to fill in the chorus behind the sound hound's big solo. Experts called it "giving mouth." Basie was the best at it you ever heard.

Dave usually hunted his dogs in a group of three. But with one of his black-and-tans tending her new pups, he had with him only Basie and Bert that night in 1920. Dave thought the hounds might find fresh possum scents in Sewell's Woods. The woods are located about ten miles from Marietta, Georgia.

He brought the pair of hounds to position under a moon that had risen above the tree line. You could hear the cicadas singing under stars dimmed by the summer moon. Still on leash, Basie and Bert lifted their noses in the air. This was a moment of prayer, it seemed to Dave. When a Coonhound sniffs, scent becomes its universe. It is a current that runs through the dog. Smell controls its breathing and its muscles, pumps its blood. The dog belongs to its nose.

In a moment, Basie and Bert flung their bodies away from Dave. He released them, and the hunt began. They always moved together, always in the same direction. One smell was the right smell, and both dogs knew the one they were after.

Dave carried a lantern in one hand, his gun in the other. He trailed behind, listening to the dogs call directions. The music had begun.

The running hounds bayed open-mouthed with long, drawn-out voices, calling Dave to come along as they rushed the trail. Dave followed the music through the woods, across a small creek, and up a sharp rise. Soon, the music changed. The dogs shortened their calling to a series of barks. The

138 *The Missing Tree*

prey was on the run. Dave couldn't see the dogs, but he followed their urgent request. He heard the barks grow sharp.

Soon, Basie took over. The prey was treed. Basie's smooth baying was slow by design. Initially, there was one sonorous call upon another. This was followed by a brief silence, during which Basie listened at regular intervals for the sound of his master's footsteps. It gave the moonlight serenade a pronounced measure of rhythm. Dave found the music intoxicating.

Bert circled the tree in frustration, reduced to whining while Basie sang both tenor and bass. Dave hurried to relieve the whining hound of her anguish. The dogs were in a low valley between two hills. The hill Dave came over was marked with a square of iron fence overgrown with vines and weeds. A family cemetery.

As Dave approached the Coonhounds, his mouth fell open. Winded from his trot with lantern and gun, he stood still to catch his breath and take it all in. He whistled to let the dogs know he was near. Knowing Dave was there, Bert was free to bark. The hounds stayed to their noisy work, circling the tree at a quickened pace.

Only there was no tree that Dave Perkins could see.

Bert hurried her circling, but in a delicate, prancing step, as if at any moment she might be forced to run or be challenged to wage war. She wagged her entire body, as was her habit, as she walked in a circle around what should have been a tree.

But there was no tree.

Basie looked straight up, ending his song, and leapt in

the air. He snarled viciously at the sky.

This was not the way Coonhounds treed a possum. It was something bigger. Dave adjusted the lantern cover for more light. Walking forward for a closer look, he heard a large crashing sound above the dogs. It sounded as if a branch had broken and was coming down through other limbs.

Basie and Bert yodeled in unison and backed up from the spot. The branch hit the ground. Dave could hear it happen, but he couldn't see a thing.

It sounded to Dave Perkins as if his dogs had treed a bear. There hadn't been bears in the woods around Marietta for decades. And of course, there was no tree. The dogs had gone mad, he thought. He was overcome with dread.

"Basie!" he called. "Bert!"

He whistled.

The Coonhounds ignored him. The hunt accounted for their inertia. They waited for Dave to join them at the bottom of the tree, to shine his light into the tree, to fire his gun. It was the sound of the gun that signaled the end of the hunt.

Dave stood his ground and held his lantern steady while his best Coonhounds circled an empty spot in the small, open valley.

A small branch snapped above the dogs. By instinct, Dave dropped the lantern and shouldered his gun. Basie and Bert backed away in unison, then as a pair leapt back to the spot. Both hounds took to growling, punctuating the guttural sounds of their threatened attack with short, sideways yaps.

Dave retrieved his lantern and ran forward. A few steps

and he stopped as an awful crashing shook the night. Whatever was in the tree that wasn't there was on its way down. It was charging the ground. It sounded as big as a bear. Even bigger.

Basie and Bert heard it coming, too. It was coming down on them. The dogs fell over backwards in their initial effort to escape. They rolled and righted themselves and took off in a dead run, away from Dave, away from the spot. They barked wildly on their mad dash. And then Dave heard the oddest sound of the night. He heard the Coonhounds hit water. He heard the splash. The dogs disappeared at the far edge of his vision, where moonlight swept the valley with a faint blur of summer mist.

Whatever was coming down the tree had stopped in midair. There wasn't another sound except the croak of a distant bullfrog. Dave stood in the spot where his beloved Coonhounds had gone mad. He walked it back and forth. He set the lantern down in the exact location Basie and Bert had believed they'd found a tree.

Dave walked the valley in the direction the hounds had taken, expecting to find a pond or a creek he hadn't known was there. There was none. And there were no dogs. He whistled for Basie and Bert. He called their names. He walked the valley twice, then again. Finally, he fired his gun in the air. That would bring them back, if anything would.

The moon moved behind the hill. His dogs were gone.

It had happened before that the hounds ran off, chasing scent, and ran so far away that Dave had to go home without them. They had returned the next day and slept for a week. However, Dave reasoned, they hadn't been chased by anything.

He told his wife about the incident, being very careful with the details. As best he could figure, his dogs had been set upon by a ghost bear, if such thing could ever exist. He knew for certain that Basie and Bert in their own hearts had something up a tree at that mysterious spot. Something up a tree that wasn't really there.

Three days later, he placed a "Dogs Lost" ad in the local paper, offering a reward for Basie and Bert's return. He mentioned Sewell's Woods and noted that any information would be helpful.

A Cherokee Indian came to the Perkins place and knocked on the door.

His name was Freeman Joshua, and he said his people had lived in the area of Sewell's Woods and that he might be able to help.

"Is that your old cemetery on the hill?" Dave asked.

"No," Freeman said. "That came later. My people lived there before your people came."

"I see," Dave said.

He eagerly agreed to Mr. Joshua's offer to help.

"Can you find the place where the dogs were lost?" Freeman asked.

Dave told him he had marked the spot, but that it didn't really matter. He could take Freeman right to it with his eyes blindfolded.

On the way to Sewell's Woods, Freeman asked the hunter every sort of detail. He was particularly interested in the crashing sounds Dave had heard.

"It sounded as big as a bear," Dave said. "A big bear. Now, there wasn't a tree, you see. But you could hear branches breaking and falling. Then you could hear the sound of it coming down the tree."

Freeman Joshua nodded. He was anxious to see the place. Dave walked him through the hunt, up the hill and past the overgrown cemetery. The Cherokee gentleman didn't give the graves a glance. But the open valley mesmerized him. He stood for the longest time staring down the gentle slope.

"This way," Dave said. "The tree is most of the way down toward that low area. I mean, the place where my dogs thought there was a tree."

Hound prints and Dave's own shoe prints well marked the place of the missing tree. Freeman squatted next to it and placed his hand on the ground. The grass and weeds were torn.

"Is there a warm spot?" Dave asked. "Can you feel anything?"

Freeman stood up. He said a few words in Cherokee and looked up at the sky.

"Where did the dogs go, Mr. Perkins?"

"That's what I'd like to know," Dave said.

"From here, I mean. Did they run straight down the rest of the slope?"

"Yes, sir, they did. Until they disappeared. I should have been able to still see them, but they disappeared. I told you about the splash, didn't I? I heard those dogs hit water, I swear. And then they were gone. And the funny thing is they stopped barking. I guess dogs do that when they swim. Come on, I'll show you. There isn't any water. Just a low area. Heck, I couldn't find a puddle."

Freeman Joshua stood in the lowest spot, where the water would have been, if there had been any. He said something in Cherokee again. This time, Dave wanted to know what.

"There is a lake here," Freeman told him. "There is a lake where we are standing. And there is a tree where your dogs were that night. I don't know how they found it, but they did."

"What do you mean? I don't see anything." Dave didn't appreciate being taken on a lark. He wanted his dogs back.

"There is a bear, Mr. Perkins. Were your dogs injured by it? Were they wounded in some way?"

"They went for a roll, they sure did. Like something gave them a whack. But I'm telling you, there was nothing there. Just a bunch of noise and two old Coonhounds caught up in madness. Maybe we should be going now."

Freeman Joshua changed his mind about trying to explain the location to Dave. It just wouldn't work.

"I'm sorry that I'm unable to help you with your dogs, Mr. Perkins. They may yet come home. I should be going now, you are right about that."

"Somebody might have taken them in," Dave surmised. "Basie and Bert are the best Coonhounds in the county."

Freeman Joshua returned often to the tree he couldn't see and walked often to the edge of the invisible lake.

The area occupied by Marietta, Georgia, was a major

city of the Cherokee. Sewell's Woods was sacred ground. Its location was forgotten among the Cherokee during the Trail of Tears.

The Cherokee respected bears above the other animals that inhabited the earth, because bears had once been human. Freeman's ancestors believed bears could speak to humans if they wanted to, but chose to talk only among themselves. There was a place in the forest where the bears gathered in late autumn before finding their winter sleeping lodges. There, the bears told each other their stories.

It was the place that the great white bear lived throughout the year. He held dominion over the bear community. He also served as an adviser and healer. He devised a way to cure a bear of any injury, even one that might otherwise prove fatal. If a bear could make its way to the place now called Sewell's Woods, it would be made well by wading into the lake.

Woodland bears once traveled to the lake through all hardships. Though many bears could no longer find their way back, Freeman understood that the lake was still there. It was an enchanted lake and could not be seen by man.

The lake also provided its curative power to all other animals of the woods, including foxes, frogs, and birds. The magic of the lake was so powerful it could even cure a man of his injuries.

But the white bear made it impossible for humans to see the lake. If they could see it, too many of them would come. They would take the lake away from the bears. Atag-Hi, the name of the lake in Cherokee, was so beautiful it could not be resisted by men were it visible to them.

An ancient Cherokee belief allows a way for the enchanted lake to be found by humans, although they will never actually see it. On rare occasions, the furious beating of thousands upon thousands of wings may be heard as waterfowl rise from the surface of the lake. It is a lake that can be heard but not seen.

In some Cherokee histories, the claim is made that the mist rising from the lake can be seen from the peaks of the hills surrounding it. But this ethereal vision occurs only in moonlight and has not been documented by the Cherokee in modern times.

Freeman Joshua knew he was blessed to have been shown the place. After much consideration, it was his decision that the sacred healing place of woodland animals should be kept to the animals themselves. Any old dog could find the place. For men, even his own children, learning the location would ruin it for all wild things.

The lake was smaller than it had once been, he imagined. Few animals could find their way to be healed because so many roads and houses had been built, so many fences. The protected trails to the enchanted lake had rapidly been erased by civilization. Freeman would hold the secret in his heart.

Dave Perkins returned home from showing the Cherokee gentleman the place where his very best Coonhounds had run off. He could have cried. There was no replacing them. No scent hound would ever sing as pretty as Basie. Dave thought he might give up on Coonhounds altogether.

It only broke your heart to love dogs as much as he did.

Then he visited the new litter. Dave sat down next to their mother, and the pups climbed all over him. He decided to keep the entire litter. No one who asks if a black-and-tan's ears are supposed to be that big should have one. Everyone knows a Coonhound flaps its ears to bring the scent to its nose.

Rose Perfume

Lufkin, Texas

Julius Gipson lived on the wrong side of the tracks in the heart of the piney woods in eastern Texas. Some would say he lived on the wrong side of life. He made more money than a lot of others did, working at the sawmill in Lufkin at the end of World War II. Julius was a dependable, hardworking man with a strong back and large, callused hands. They say that after your first year of working in a sawmill, you don't get splinters. You give them.

In his personal life, Julius had a weakness for soft things. He spent all his money on women, bringing home one after another. As Julius got older, people noticed the women he brought home got younger. He met them in the bars in town. If you asked Julius if he was married, he would say he was. There was a houseful of children, after all. And there was always a woman in the house. But Julius was never married in the written-down-on-paper sort of way.

One day, Julius found himself a young woman he wanted to keep. Miranda was the prettiest of all. And she always smelled of rose perfume. He brought her home and asked her to stay.

"You stay here and make biscuits and gravy," Julius told her, "and I'll buy you everything you want."

Miranda wanted a car.

This pretty lady could cook. But it didn't take her half the day, and she didn't like sitting around.

"When am I going to get a car?" she asked Julius.

Miranda wanted to go places. She wanted to sneak out of the house and go someplace where she could dress up. She wanted to dance. There were places around Lufkin where the bars played music in the middle of the day. These were establishments she was familiar with. They kept dark curtains on the windows, and it was just like night inside in the middle of the afternoon. Miranda figured she could go out dancing and be home by the time Julius came in from work. If she had a car.

"Why don't you make some quilts for the children,"

Julius said, "and I'll buy you everything you want."

Miranda cut up his old pants worn out from his work in the sawmill and made them into quilts. There was one for each of the children's beds.

"When do we get a car?" she asked Julius after the quilts were made.

"Pretty soon," he told her. He scratched his chin a little. Julius was saving his money as fast as he could. "But those quilts are pretty small, you see. They barely cover the bed. What we need to keep the children warm are quilts that come down all the way to the floor."

Miranda cut up an old suit that didn't fit Julius anymore and made the quilts bigger. When she was done, her fingers were sore. She'd had enough of quilt making, she decided. It was time for Julius to buy her a car.

"If you don't buy me a car," Miranda said, "I'll be leaving you, Julius. And I'll take those quilts with me. I don't want you and any other woman sleeping under them."

"Hush, now," Julius said. "Those quilts are the children's. And I don't want no other woman unless it's you."

Julius figured he was getting too old to attract the pretty girls. He figured the next woman he brought home, if Miranda left him, would be ugly. And she wouldn't smell of rose perfume. He sure didn't want that.

Julius also figured Miranda wanted a car to run around on him some. Young women were like that. Especially the pretty ones. But he took Miranda at her word about leaving him if he didn't bring a car home fast. So he did. He bought a big, black car from a man in town.

The first thing you know, Miranda wasn't staying home anymore. Julius thought about it all day at work and all day the next day, too. He came up with the perfect plan.

Julius had one of his friends from the sawmill come and drive the car to the front of the house around midnight. His friend lay down in the front seat, where he couldn't be seen through the windows on either side of the car, or from the front or back either. Then he honked the horn. He blew the horn and blew the horn. And just kept blowing it.

Julius and Miranda came out on the porch and stared at the honking car. It drove off while they watched. His friend had learned how to drive the car a ways without ever sitting up. Some of the neighbors came out and saw it, too.

Julius took a big breath of her rose perfume and told Miranda the car was haunted by a ghost.

She believed it because that car came later to the back of the house and honked its horn until she came to the window and looked.

"It's a ghost, sure is," Julius told her.

The neighbors all agreed.

Miranda couldn't be driving a car that was haunted. It would kill her if she did. She stayed home all day like before, only she hated it more than when she first moved in. It vexed her mind.

Miranda caught a headache that threw her to bed, flat on her back, and that's where she stayed all day. It was horrible headache, she told Julius. She quit putting on her perfume and lipstick. She couldn't do the cooking. She couldn't do the washing or the ironing. She couldn't do anything all night either, except lie still.

At first, Julius thought she was making it up, but the headache was real. It lasted longer than anyone could fake a headache. She was as sick as a dog. And Miranda never even mentioned the car.

Julius climbed out of bed in the middle of the darkest night, when there was no moon. He went outside and sat in the chair on his front porch, pondering what to do.

He couldn't think of anything, so he prayed. Julius Gipson prayed to his dead momma for help. She knew how to fix people's sicknesses, always had. If she could help people on earth, there was no reason she couldn't do a little something from heaven. Leastways for her very own kin.

"Oh, Lord," he said, "how's things in heaven? They're mighty frightful down Texas way. If you don't mind, I was sort of wondering if I could speak to my mother a minute."

Julius waited. He didn't know how long it would take Him to find the right cloud.

"Now, Momma, if you're up there, won't you please do something to ease the situation?" He said *please* as pretty as he knew how, as pretty as rose perfume. "You know I've worked hard, Momma. I've always worked hard."

Prayer is a powerful tool. When Julius went back to bed to get his sleep for the next day's work at the sawmill, Miranda slipped out of the covers. She could barely stand up from her headache. But she walked through the house step by careful step, past the children's beds, outside to the front porch. The fresh air, she thought, might relieve the misery in her head a little bit.

Miranda felt a puff of wind on her face. It was warm, like someone's breath.

She felt the wind again, this time on her hand. Then that circle of wind lifted her hand in front of her and tugged on her wrist. Soon, that puff of wind was pulling her along into the yard. Miranda followed it as if she were being led by a guide.

She tripped only once, on some toy one of the children had left outside. When she came to the backyard, the wind stopped. Sitting under the only tree out back was a big white dog with a blue-and-white checkered handkerchief on her head. Miranda could see the dog plain as day. And the dog could see her, too.

The dog pointed at the checkered handkerchief with one of her paws, and Miranda walked to the dog and took the handkerchief off her head. Inside the handkerchief was a bunch of pills. Miranda swallowed one, and as soon as she did, her headache went away. And as soon as she swallowed that pill, the dog began to talk.

The dog told her people get to be big white dogs when they die. When they have anything to do on earth, that is. Then the dog explained things about the current situation. She explained things to Miranda in plain terms, like all dogs do when you can understand what they're saying.

Miranda could stay home and raise the children, and everything would be the same as before the headache came.

Well, Miranda figured the children weren't hers anyway. And if she couldn't drive the car, then Julius was just too old for her. She didn't want to go back to the way it was.

The dog understood all this, having been around the block a few times herself. She told Miranda there were other choices. What Miranda didn't realize was that the pill had changed her into a dog. That's how she was able to understand what this dog was telling her. But she didn't have a mirror on her at the time.

Miranda could leave if she wanted to, the dog said, but she would have to keep taking the pills the dog gave her. That first pill would wear off, and Miranda would be just fine for a while. Everything would be normal, but the headache would come back and drop her to all fours. The only cure was to take one of those pills again or live with Julius. If she stayed with Julius, she wouldn't need the pills at all. That was the deal. Lickety-split, the dog was gone.

Miranda selected her choice. The next morning, she put on her lipstick and her rose perfume. She wrapped the pills back into the blue-and-white checkered handkerchief, folded it neatly, tucked it inside her purse, and left Julius and the children behind. She was gone, she thought, for good.

Julius mourned his loss. He moaned for a week or more every night when he went to bed alone. Her pillow still smelled like rose perfume. Smelling roses, he moaned loud and he moaned low. His was the saddest moaning Julius had ever heard. He was mighty upset by the sounds. He couldn't sleep at all. His work suffered at the sawmill, and they were likely to fire him if he didn't do better soon. Either that or he'd end up sawing his hand off. If that happened, the moaning would only get worse, he figured. He

might even have to holler some.

Now, there wasn't another woman who could replace Miranda, not in all of Texas. But the children needed a woman in the house, and so did he. So Julius knocked the sawdust off his clothes. He combed his hair and brushed his teeth.

He drove his car all over Lufkin, looking high and looking low, this side of the tracks and that. He looked in all the bars, checking the rows of barstools for a woman he could bring home. When a barstool was empty, Julius would sit down on it to see if it felt warm, to see if a woman had been sitting there he might have just missed. He'd sit there for a time, and the moaning would start again, and he'd have to get up and check the dance floor.

Julius went to the men's room. On his way back to see if anyone new was on a barstool, he met a woman named Mae leaning in the corner behind the pool table. He tapped her on the shoulder and showed Mae his money. She said Julius could ask her anything he wanted to. He told her he needed a woman at home for the children and such. Mae came home with him.

The first night come wintertime that it got real cold, Julius put one of Miranda's handmade quilts on the bed and climbed in under the covers with Mae. They got snuggly together, and pretty soon Julius was warm from his head to his toes. Every so often, he had to lift one corner of the covers with his big toe to let some of the warmth out. So he was surprised when later in the night he woke up with the shivers.

The quilt was gone.

Julius hopped out of bed and walked around to Mae's side, expecting to find the quilt on the floor. It wasn't there. He turned the lamp on to try to find it. Mae woke up when all the light hit her face.

"Whatever are you looking for?" she asked Julius, who was on his hands and knees poking around under the iron bed.

"The covers," he said.

"They aren't here," Mae told him. "Your dog come and pulled the quilt off the bed and dragged it out of the room."

"I don't have a dog."

"I saw it, Julius."

"There isn't a dog to see," Julius said.

"But I saw it, I sure did."

Julius gave up finding the quilt. He put on two pairs of socks and went back to bed. He got under the sheet that about had holes in it, it was worn so thin. He curled up close to Mae to keep his teeth from chattering. His elbows were cold. And his nose felt like someone had stuck an ice cube on his face. He was able, just barely, to go back to sleep.

In the morning, he found the quilt on one of the children's beds. It touched the floor on either side.

That night, he put the big quilt on the iron bed and went to snoring. But he woke up cold again. The cover was gone. It was as if his cut-up old pants had learned to walk on their own with nobody's legs inside of them.

Mae was wide awake the whole time.

"It was that dog again," she said.

Julius would have believed her if he had a dog.

"If there was a dog in here, it must have been a ghost," Julius finally said, trying to figure the whole thing out.

This troubled Mae to a bothersome degree. She didn't believe she could live in a house that had a ghost dog pulling the covers off the bed. An old man who snored all the time wasn't worth being hexed by a ghost, even if he did have a good job at the sawmill and brought home plenty of food for her to eat.

Mae left Julius. She went back to leaning in the corner behind the pool table at the bar, waiting for another man to come out of the restroom, tap her on the shoulder, and ask her a question or two. Whatever the question was, Mae said yes, as long as the man promised there was no ghost walking around his house, pulling on the covers or rattling the doors.

Julius Gipson was tired of bringing home women. The children were big enough to take care of themselves. The oldest one knew how to cook, and she made sure the other ones went to school. He would save a little money for the kids, he thought, and live alone until he was old enough to die.

Julius put the big quilt on the bed, and it stayed there the whole night. As long as he slept alone, the quilt stayed put. Miranda's pillow still smelled like rose perfume, even though another woman had been sleeping on it. He missed Miranda all over again and took to moaning. He should have let her drive the car, Julius thought. He moaned some more.

He moaned so much he finally got used to it. Julius learned to sleep and moan at the same time. Moaning was easier to sleep through than chattering teeth. Julius was sad at night, but it was better than freezing in your sleep. He was lonely when he went to bed, and he was lonely when he got up in the morning, but at least he was warm.

After a week or two, Julius wasn't quite as lonely as he was before.

A pretty white dog showed up at the house one night to keep him company. It came inside when the children opened the door. Julius got out of bed to look it over. It wasn't a ghost dog. Julius made sure of that. It was as real as any dog and had thick, white fur.

He checked it over carefully. The only thing different about the dog was it had small red marks on the tops of its front paws. Its feet hadn't been cut or hurt in any way. It was as if someone had spilled a bit of red ink on the white fur growing out of the dog's front paws. Julius fed the dog and gave it water. It was good with the kids, so he let it stay.

The children named the dog Eskimo. Late at night, most of the time well after Julius had gone to sleep, the dog would get up on the bed with him. Eskimo curled up on the pillow next to his and went right to sleep. It was there in the morning when he woke up to get dressed and go to work.

He wasn't as lonely as he once was. Some nights, he went to sleep without remembering to moan. He dreamed of Miranda and could smell her rose perfume in his sleep. Julius felt fine about that. A man could live without a woman just fine, if he had a dog.

Sundays, he and the children would take Eskimo riding in the car.

That was the end of the story, as far as Julius was concerned. But there was a taxi driver in Nacogdoches who had a different story to tell. Nobody ever believed it, but he told it just the same, how on a Saturday night back in the forties, he picked up a fare. A woman in a white fur hat flagged him down in front of one of the all-night-dancing bars. She wore lipstick and rose perfume. She was the prettiest woman he'd ever seen. She told him where she needed to go. She had the number of the house and the name of the street, but it was in another town than Nacogdoches.

"I don't have the time to drive that far," the taxi man said. "Company won't let me drive you out of town without I have permission first."

"That's the silliest thing I ever heard. I've taken the taxi from Dallas to home before. The driver was very kind, and I tipped him well."

She crossed her legs and waited. The driver looked at her in the mirror. She crossed her legs the other way. He decided the woman was the generous type. He drove out of town.

The woman in the backseat took off her shoes.

"I've been dancing for hours and hours," she said. "My little pups are sore."

Soon, they were on the highway, where there were no streetlights. They headed south. It was as dark in the back of the taxi as if you had closed a door. The cabdriver swore he heard the woman unzip her dress, but he couldn't see for sure. He could feel her squirming around back there. Her dress rustled pretty loud, and he thought she might be getting it off of her.

"Don't be taking your dress off now, you hear?" he said, glancing over his shoulder for a better glimpse.

To his surprise, she was lying down on the seat, as best he could tell. It didn't seem right to him that a pretty woman would take her clothes off in the back of a cab and go to bed. It didn't seem right at all. So he drove a little faster. And a little faster still.

He got to Lufkin fairly quick and began looking for the address. Driving under the streetlights, he glanced into the backseat, and the dress was there, all right, but the woman was all scrunched up down on the floorboard. He couldn't see her at all, just the top of the white cap she wore.

The dress kept rustling as he drove. He was anxious now to drop off the fare and drive back to Nacogdoches before he might be caught leaving town without getting permission from the company. He found the address, parked the cab, and told her how much she owed. She didn't saying anything.

When he looked in the backseat, the dress was gone and the woman was still hiding on the floor. He figured it was a bad sign and hopped out of the cab and opened the back door. The driver tried to scream and holler at the same time. But all he did was swallow his breath. He nearly drowned on it.

A white dog jumped out of the cab. It had a green dress rolled up in its mouth and a shoe poking out either end of the roll. The dog ran up to the house.

The driver, the way he told the story, didn't stick around to see who lived there. He didn't want to know. He jumped in the driver's seat and drove like the devil all the way to Nacogdoches. He found three dollars in the backseat of his cab when he got there. The bills were a little damp at the edges, and he bet that dog had them in its mouth. It was more than twice the fare, though, and that was good enough for the driver.

Miranda put away her clothes and went to bed. She wiped the lipstick from her mouth.

Julius, snoring away next to her, smelled rose perfume in his sleep.

Once she'd spent some time with him, Miranda would be normal again, and she could leave the house for a little fun.

The pretty woman had overlooked one thing when she made her choice to leave Julius Gipson and go dancing with younger men. The pills ran out. She always came home again.

Woods and Sea

Suwannee, Florida

Islands are numerous where the Suwannee River empties into the Gulf of Mexico high on the Florida Panhandle. The Lower Suwannee National Wildlife Refuge extends for miles north and south of the estuary, encircling the small town of Suwannee, Florida.

The majority of the refuge is very low, flat, and easily flooded. The slight changes of elevation and the proximity to both salt and fresh water create an unusual diversity of wildlife habitats, including flood-plain hardwoods, cypress-lined sloughs, freshwater marshes, salt and brackish marshes, cabbage-palm and cedar-tree islands, hardwood hammocks, cypress domes, and low pinewoods.

The refuge is host to a variety of migratory birds, including many different species of wading birds and shore-birds. Swallow-tailed kites, ospreys, and bald eagles also nest on the refuge.

The river and its coastal estuary are an important habitat for Florida's dwindling population of manatees, sadly in danger of extinction. Mariners, perhaps too busy to take but a glance, once thought the manatee was a mermaid. Close up, the manatee's bulky appearance is a far cry from the fabled slinky mermaid of mariner lore. Manatees are truly unique, docile creatures that can live in both salt and fresh water. They are sometimes called "sea cows" because they eat grass. The mammal's closest living relative is the elephant. Most are gray or brown. They can grow as long as thirteen feet and as heavy as two thousand pounds. That would be one whale of a mermaid.

An exception to the flat, marshy terrain is a large shell mound in the refuge, a prehistoric site where indigenous people built up the swampy ground to a height of twenty-eight feet above sea level by stacking discarded seashells, crab shells, and the like.

Scientists estimate that shell mounding in Florida began as early as 2500 B.C. Mixed in with the shells are various bones, artifacts, and pottery. However, archaeologists have yet to come to a complete understanding of these extremely early settlements.

At the shell mound near Suwannee, recent scientific prodding has uncovered the entire skeleton of a large dog at a depth of twelve feet. This small portion of the mound appears to have been redug in the late 1700s or early 1800s, perhaps by a pioneer Florida family hoping to erect a home in an area of the Florida coast where most dwellings are on stilts. Because the original strata of the shell mound had been disturbed, the scientists abandoned their probe of this site. Interested in the chronology of prehistoric Florida Indians, and not at all intrigued by a few pieces of wood planking left by a pioneer family only two or three hundred years ago, the archaeologists moved to other shell mounds in the state to conduct their field research.

One Florida historian believes the pioneer family who came to this shell mound was that of Harold Goodwin Pease, a wealthy planter who moved to the Gulf coast of Florida to establish a large sugar plantation inland. Before the days of the railroad, plantations shipped their crops by boat. Pease brought his family to the mouth of the Suwannee, a location where he could oversee the shipping of his sugar crop and provide his wife and daughters with access to sea travel.

Most of the islands south along the coast toward Cedar Key are low-lying and surrounded by extremely shallow sand, mud, or grass flats. These are excellent crabbing locations. Tiny Garden Island is one of the many places throughout the area where a mermaid ghost has been seen. She is, by all accounts, much smaller than a manatee.

A recent sighting was documented in 1998, when a husband and wife staying on Garden Island were called by the insistent barking of their dog to get out of bed. Their small boat was tied at the southern end of the island, where a sea channel kept the vessel from resting on mud at low tide. Leaving their beds, they walked down to the channel to see if someone else had brought a boat to the island.

"It was a romantic time in our lives," the wife said. "I remember that my husband and I were holding hands. Suddenly, he stopped walking and squeezed my hand tightly. Our boat had come into view. I stopped, too, and stared at the boat."

A woman with long hair was sitting on the bow of their boat. She was bathed in shimmering moonlight reflected from the sea.

"As we watched, the woman slipped forward and, without a splash, disappeared into the sea," she recalled. "I remember thinking that she was beautiful, but I'm not sure how I knew that. As soon as she went underwater, our dog stopped barking."

This was not the first time a ghost of a woman had been seen occupying small boats in the area. Throughout the low islands and even into the mouth of the Suwannee River, recreational boaters have returned to their launches from a visit to land to see a woman sitting on their boats. She slips back into the water when seen. Persistent rumor has made of her a mermaid.

Other times, the ghost is known to walk from the sea onto an island where a dog is barking. She walks as if her feet are tied, seeming to float along the marshes. She emerges from the water fully erect and comes ashore. She is never seen to swim. She is not a mermaid. Taking her leave of the grassy shore, the ghost drifts slowly away, as if she might be walking upon the water.

It is local legend that sailors who bring along a dog on their watercraft, as many recreational boaters do, are certain to see this ghost at twilight if they are still upon the water. She is never seen pulling herself onto a boat. Rather, she arrives sitting on the bow, staring in the direction of the nearest landfall.

A separate female ghost haunts the Lower Suwannee National Wildlife Refuge as well.

Janie Robinson and her husband, setting crab traps near the shell mound, managed to mire their boat in deep mud. It was a night of a full moon, and the tide was exceptionally low. While her husband worked to free the boat, Janie slipped away to answer the call of nature at the edge of the sparse woods that have come to encircle the shell mound in recent decades. Screaming in fear, Janie soon ran from the woods. Behind her stood a woman in a long dress, accompanied by a large dog. The woman, as reported by Joyce Elson Moore in her book, *Haunt Hunter's Guide to Florida*, appeared to be walking on air about a foot above the ground.

On another occasion, a close friend of Janie's was at the shell mound waiting for her husband to finish crabbing. She was with her eight-year-old daughter, who at one point began walking purposefully toward the woods. The girl's mother instructed her to come back immediately. But her daughter kept walking. The young mother ran to catch up to her daughter and, reaching her, saw a woman in a long dress standing at the edge of the woods. Once again, the lady in the woods was accompanied by a large dog.

The dog is named Hamilton, and it was his skeleton archaeologists uncovered at the shell mound. An Irish Wolfhound, Hamilton was the guardian and companion pet of sisters Gwendolyn and Addie Pease.

At a time when pirates regularly plied the waters off the Gulf coast of Florida, the sisters found themselves alone when word was carried to them by other settlers that a trio of masted ships under the command of Benicio Materros was making its way toward the islands. Their mother had recently died of fever. Their father, traveling inland on the Suwannee River to oversee labor at his sugar plantation, would not return for several days. The sisters' house servants and the hired caretaker quickly abandoned the shell mound upon hearing that pirate ships were in the area. A small boat remained for Gwendolyn and Addie, should they decide to follow the example of their servants.

What would their father say if they abandoned their home because ships were sailing by?

"There's no reason for pirates to come to land here," Gwendolyn said. She was the older of the two. "The servants will return tomorrow."

Addie, the more adventuresome of the sisters, was excited by the prospect of seeing pirates.

Hamilton, being a rough-coated, powerfully built Wolfhound, wasn't afraid of pirates. Taller than a Mastiff and bred for hunting, shaggy-browed Wolfhounds aren't afraid of anyone. A gentle and amiable companion of the family, Hamilton proved fierce when provoked.

In the morning, Addie found her father's small brass telescope in his desk and carried it with her in a large front pocket of her dress. If the ships were visible when the mist lifted, perhaps she would see Benicio Materros himself standing on deck. A pretender to royalty, Materros was said to wear a purple satin sash across his chest. He would be easy to pick out from the others.

Addie and Gwendolyn stood on the shell mound with Hamilton, watching the ships tack toward them. The smallest of the vessels maintained speed and made its way into the mouth of the Suwannee River, the sisters' escape route. Still, they could not believe the pirates were coming to the shell mound. There was nothing here for pirates.

"Is that the flag of Portugal?" Addie asked her sister, handing her the brass telescope.

Gwendolyn held the scope to her eye.

"I can't tell. It might be Spain."

"Look over both decks," Addie instructed. "Can you see the men yet? Is one wearing a purple sash?"

Gwendolyn gasped.

"They've dropped anchor," she said, handing the scope to her sister. "The sails are coming down."

The pirates lowered shore boats into the water. They were coming to the shell mound. Benicio Materros had not been to the location in more than seven years. He had no idea a home had been established there. The shell mound provided a visible landmark. Elevated as it was, it also provided a perfect place for hiding a large portion of his treasure, where it would be protected from storms and tides when he departed to sail along the northern Gulf coast. There, he might find the opportunity to raid small port villages and lone sea vessels.

As the pirates rowed toward shore, Addie and Gwendolyn rushed to load items of value into their small craft. They would chance escape by sea, afraid of the smallest pirate vessel, anchored at the mouth of the Suwannee. Their plan was to move clandestinely southward, between the Suwannee Sound and Hog Island. At the tip of the sound, they could turn their boat quickly back on the tide and come under an extended finger of land and be hidden until the pirates set sail. Once around the tip of the sound, they would not be seen.

They rescued their father's books and papers from his desk. Several pieces of silver service, including their mother's beloved teapot, were wrapped in mosquito netting taken from the beds. Gwendolyn retrieved a small wooden box of gold coins. Addie collected what jewelry the family possessed. Hamilton climbed in and out of the boat as the sisters loaded items.

Soon, but not soon enough, everything was ready. Sitting side by side, the sisters each took an oar. Gwendolyn pushed against the bank with hers to launch the craft. At that moment, upon hearing the voices of pirates as they came ashore on the other side of the shell mound, Hamilton leapt from the boat and galloped away. He loped onto and across the shell mound to greet the visitors, whose arrival he might have mistaken for that of Harold Goodwin Pease and his party.

No more than a few feet from shore, but safely into the water, the sisters' boat sat idle, both oars lifted.

"We must leave him," Gwendolyn said.

"No," Addie said, making up her mind. "He'll come to me."

She clambered over her sister, rocking the boat. Half standing, half falling, the younger sister flung herself to land.

Materros sent armed parties in two directions along the shore. Their purpose was to secure the area and see if any errant alligators from the Suwannee were in a position to menace the pirates' endeavors. Materros hated and feared alligators above all things. He possessed a deep-seated desire to never be outfitted with a wooden leg.

Other pirates unloaded the boats of four wooden chests wrapped in chains.

Wearing his purple sash, a sword and scabbard at his belt, Materros strode inland to the shell mound, followed by four sailors carrying trenching tools. Materros held a black-powder pistol in his hand and had a matching weapon in his belt.

Hamilton stood in the middle of the vast shell mound. A sight hound, he could now easily see that the pirates were not people he knew. Instinctually, he was aware of danger. Addie whispered his name from the far side of the mound. Hamilton could hear her plainly, his small ears twitching as he judged her distance without turning his steady gaze from the approaching men. He was also aware that other men were circling the mound. In an instant, the Wolfhound understood that the men were adversaries.

With Addie at his back and Gwendolyn farther behind, Hamilton's job was no longer that of amiable companion. It was that of protector. He barked once, then growled. It was a warning.

The pirates heard him and were at once still where they stood. No one spoke. Materros drew his second pistol and resumed walking. The sailors with him dropped their trenching tools and produced a variety of weapons from their clothing.

Addie was terrified. She came onto the shell mound, trying to lure Hamilton from his pose of attack.

Deep-chested, long-legged, and muscular, Hamilton had a job to do. His ears folded to the back of his broad head. He showed his teeth. The crush of a Wolfhound's powerful jaws is greater than that of even a wolf. It can bite through a man's leg in a single snap, breaking bone. There are few adversaries a Wolfhound cannot quickly conquer. Hamilton had no fear of men.

Materros appeared on the shell mound. Addie saw his purple sash.

Hamilton, with a commanding leap, galloped toward the pirate in full attack.

Addie, her heart stung by this action, could not stop herself from running after her beloved pet.

"No!" she cried as Materros fired a fatal shot into the charging dog.

Hamilton collapsed at his feet, dead when he fell. Materros barely glanced at the animal. He raised his other pistol to Addie. She stood still in the middle of the shell mound, her hands flung to her face to ease the roar of the pulse in her ears.

Materros came slowly forward, his sailors appearing to either side.

Addie's heart was broken by instant dread and terror, by grief and fear. Tears ran down her face. Her heart pounded in its cage. Suddenly, and by surprise, Addie was overcome with anger, an anger she could not control. Her hand shaking badly, she removed a small dagger from her dress pocket. It was the knife from her father's desk. Adrenaline spurred her muscles, heating the skin on her arms and legs.

She rushed Materros. She meant to bury the small knife in the middle of his purple sash.

One of the sailors laughed. As he had with the dog, Materros waited until she was close to him, until he could see her eyes blurred red with tears. He fired his other pistol. The lead ball flew through her breast, her heart. Annie dropped to her knees, her mouth open, her arm held out. When her arm dropped, she was dead.

One of the armed parties of pirates captured Gwendolyn, who swung her oar wildly at the men to protect herself. One of them stepped into the water and overturned her small boat. Two others dragged her to shore. One retrieved a loose bag of mosquito netting from the water. It held service items of solid silver. The small box of gold coins and jewelry, along with Harold Goodwin

Pease's books and papers, were lost to the mud at the bottom of the waterway.

The pirates canvassed the area, trooping farther inland than they preferred. No one else was there. Addie's body was carried to the house, which was emptied of all portable things of value, including the cooking pans. The plundering sailors found favor with the women's clothing, arguing endlessly over satin ribbon and lace. The house was set afire and burned to the ground.

Once the pit in the shell mound was twenty feet deep, well above sea level but too far down to be discovered by accident, wooden planks were arranged to form its bottom. Lead sheeting was placed on top of that, and the four chests followed. More planking followed that. The hole was filled in with the dug shells to a level of perhaps twelve feet when Materros had his men stop their work.

"Put in the dog," he commanded. "It will guard our treasure better than the ghost of a sailor."

Hamilton's body was placed into the pit, and the hole was filled in entirely. The pirates returned to their waiting ships in darkness. Gwendolyn was taken aboard the captain's vessel. The anchors were lifted. The ships would find morning a fair distance from shore. The smallest ship came from the river's mouth to sea under the sparkling of a million stars.

Gwendolyn was put in leg shackles, a small link of chain holding her ankles close. On deck, she was shown to Materros. He instructed that she not be taken below. He did not want her becoming sick. She was valuable cargo and would be bartered.

"Feed her," he said. "Then we'll see what we do."

Gwendolyn could not eat. Neither could she face her fate at the hands of pirates. She prayed for her sister's soul and flung herself overboard when no one expected she might. Her ankles in irons, she sank immediately. Her eyes closed, Gwendolyn said goodbye to everything as her body moved downward into the salty darkness of the sea.

She's there still. And she's searching.

Drowning is a lonely death. Gwendolyn's ghost is attracted to the barking of dogs. She comes from the sea as a mermaid might, but she is not looking for sailors. She is searching for her home, which is no longer there. Gwendolyn Pease is lured by dogs barking, believing it might be that of her Wolfhound, Hamilton.

Hamilton spends his eternity at Addie's side, walking silently through the woods encircling the shell mound in the Lower Suwannee National Wildlife Refuge.

It has been reported that a treasure hunter from St. Petersburg found portions of antique wooden chests in the vicinity of the shell mound. It is not known what else he found.

Devil Dog

Cedar Cliff, North Carolina

Cedar Cliff rises above the Tuckasegee River in one of the more remote mountain areas of western North Carolina. Here, rushing creeks bring their water to the river from the fall of steep ridges on the southern side of Rich Mountain, a narrow range of rocky altitudes topped to the northeast by Rough Butt Bald. Isolated populations, the descendants of pioneer families, have built their cabin homes in the deep mountain coves.

No one lived on Cedar Cliff, not since the War Between the States. The little mountain was haunted by devil dogs. Large, black hounds rushed from behind the trees and chased off anyone who had any sense at all. There were once five such dogs on Cedar Cliff. By the early 1930s, however, there was only one left.

An old woman lived in a cabin near Cedar Cliff. Annie still sang the English ballads she'd heard as a child, songs carved in the hearts and memories of mountain mothers since long before Annie was born. She sang the songs as she learned them, not as they might be written down in books somewhere. Her favorites were "Barbry Allen," "William Riley," and "Pretty Saro."

Annie told mountain stories passed down in her family. Stories of panthers screaming in the night outside the cabin door. Stories of love and murder. She also told what were known then as "Why Stories." They were older than the ballads. Why Stories were legends sometimes told to children to explain things.

Annie's stories came to the attention of a university folklore professor, who traveled to her cabin to hear them firsthand and write them down before Annie died. She was in her seventies then.

Why Stories are sometimes short and sometimes long.
Why do dogs have black lips?
Because they rescued the cows' teats when the grass

caught fire, and it burned their muzzles.

Why do dogs chase cats?

"Because," Annie said, "a long time ago, they were husband and wife." She threw back her head and laughed.

The professor wrote it down. Annie spoke with the clipped Southern accent peculiar to the mountains, saying some of her vowels from the back of her throat.

"That's the short version," she said. "The real reason takes longer to hear, if you have the time."

"I'm all ears," the professor said. "Take your time, and don't leave out anything."

"You ever see a writer what doesn't have both his ears?" Annie asked.

"No, I don't think so," her visitor replied.

Annie nodded solemnly.

"What some people say around here is that every time a writer tells the truth, one of his ears falls off."

It took the professor a moment to understand the joke. He stopped writing and smiled at Annie.

She grinned back at him, her eyes twinkling.

"The real reason dogs chase cats," Annie said. "Is that the one you want to hear?"

The professor nodded, putting his pencil to paper again.

Annie told the whole thing.

There was man from the Tuckasegee who made moonshine. His place was somewhere along Caney Fork, Annie said. She didn't know the man's name, but he was getting on in years, and his bones were knotted up something awful. He couldn't hoe the corn anymore, and you need corn to make shine. He didn't have any money put away.

He was feeling pretty bad about it and started in drinking the shine he hadn't sold off to his neighbors yet. When he drank the last of the last jug, he lay in his yard all night and moaned. You could hear him from everywhere.

"Oh, the little people in the woods here around can't tolerate someone moaning like that," Annie said.

The little people were magic, she explained. No one ever really saw one, but they were there.

"Lo, if a fairy didn't come along and put an amber-colored jewel in the empty jug so the man would stop moaning."

The amber jewel was magic. It was actually a small piece of hardened moonlight. It kept the jug from ever going empty again. There was always moonshine when that jewel was in the jug. The old man didn't have to grow corn anymore. He didn't have to build a fire and cook mash to make his shine. He just poured it from that jug. He started selling liquor again.

"But you had to bring your own cup," Annie said. "He'd fill it up for you from that jug with a jewel in it. Lordy, it was good shine." She smacked her lips and smiled at the professor.

"Now, this fellow had him a dog and a cat. He made them guard the jug at night when he went to sleep. What he didn't know was that the dog and the cat fell asleep, too. They just acted real alert and all till that old man went to bed. Then the cat fell asleep. And the dog got sleepy and started yawning, watching the cat snoozing away like that.

First one eye closed, then the other. You know, they were both asleep in a few minutes."

That morning when the old man woke up, he discovered the jug was empty. There wasn't a drop. The jewel was gone. He looked inside the jug with one eye, then the other. He turned the jug upside down and gave it a mighty shake. Nothing.

His luck had run dry.

The old man thought he must have poured the little piece of amber into some customer's Mason jar and hadn't noticed it.

The dog and cat knew better. They felt bad about the situation. That night, they talked it over and decided to search for the jewel.

The dog and cat slept during the day, taking short naps whenever they could, and searched at night. They walked everywhere. The dog would sniff around the bushes and trees and dig holes in the ground. People would get up in the morning and find holes in their yards. The cat climbed on the roofs and looked in all the chimneys.

One night, the cat smelled shine inside a cabin he'd climbed onto. The cat smelled it coming up the chimney. It smelled that amber jewel, too. It was inside the house. The cat came back down and told the dog, and they came up with a plan.

The dog went to the front door and started barking. When the people came out to see what was the matter, the cat went down the chimney, found the jewel sitting on a dresser, and carried it off.

181

"Now, this old cabin was on the other side of the river," Annie said.

The dog had swum it the night before with the cat on its back. But it was broad daylight when they came to the Tuckasegee on their way home. The cat put the jewel in its mouth and climbed on the dog's back. It held on tight as the dog jumped into the water and started swimming.

There were children playing at the edge of the Tuckasegee. They'd never seen a dog swim across the river with a cat on its back, and they started laughing.

"The little girls and the little boys laughed and laughed," Annie said.

The dog didn't think anything was funny. But the cat did. The cat started laughing, just a little at first. Then it laughed so hard the amber jewel fell from its mouth. The dog heard it hit the water, *ka-plunk*, and it dove after the jewel.

It dove deep. The cat, hanging on in terror at being submerged, clawed deep into the dog's neck. The dog was in great pain from the cat's claws and had to hurry and find the jewel, which it did. It got the amber jewel in its mouth and shot to the surface like a flash. It growled all the way across the river, blood coming from the holes in its skin.

When the dog swam ashore, it was mad at the cat. It leapt for the cat, which ran up the nearest tree, where it arched its back, spitting river water. The cat, nearly drowned, had to spit out the water to get its breath.

"That's why cats spit at dogs and why dogs chase cats," Annie said.

The professor wrote down the ending, then waited for Annie to continue. But that was all of the story, the way she knew it.

"Did the old man get the jewel back?" the professor finally asked.

"I reckon," Annie said. "They're still selling shine at Caney Fork, ain't they?"

She grinned.

"Have you been down to the Tuckasegee and looked at it?"

The professor said he had.

"Now, that's a real pretty river. When that water runs over the rocks, it sings. You go down there and listen to it. That's the singingest river you ever saw."

Annie stopped talking for a spell. She stared off into the trees that surrounded her place. Some of the tall trees she had planted herself. She was older than the trees, she realized. She was seventy-eight years old. She wouldn't last much longer. People don't.

"These mountains are full of dog stories," she said. "I know a better one. Over there at Cedar Cliff is a devil dog. He roams the place, and he won't end until I do. You see, I'm the last one. There was a dog for each of us. And I'm the last one."

The professor had heard a rumor about ghost dogs on Cedar Cliff, but he'd never heard the story behind it.

Annie decided to tell him the story. It wasn't a Why Story. It was her story, and it was the truth.

"In 1865, when I was twelve or thirteen, Yankee soldiers

came into the mountains here around to force rules on us at the end of the war. The war was ending for sure, but it wasn't all over yet, you understand. Them Yankees acted like it was. They acted like we had elected them to tell us what to do.

"My daddy was dead. He was killed in the war, and there wasn't anything my momma hated more than a Yankee soldier. You see, they wore their uniforms and carried their guns and told us what to do. They made us feed them and feed their horses, too. They took our livestock. They moved right into people's homes, and the people had to move into the barn."

Annie closed her eyes while she talked.

"I can see them now. There were three of them that formed a little group and camped up on Cedar Cliff. Now, these three were meaner than the others. They came down to the houses where the men were gone from. Some of the men weren't home because they were prisoners of war. Others were dead on the battlefield.

"These soldiers, these three, were trying to make the women do what they wanted, and the women didn't want to. There were children in the homes, but the women were widows, the ones the soldiers picked out. They picked on the widow women.

"My mother was one of them. There were others I know of. And I was twelve or thirteen then, and the soldiers came to our home, and one of them wanted to dance with me. He stood me up and walked around the room with me like music was playing. My toes were touching the floor, but he moved me around like I didn't weigh a pound.

"Well, that was all my mother could take.

"You see, with the menfolk gone to war, the women had learned things they had to do when no man was there to do it for them. They chopped wood, they sure did. And they hunted. Maybe they just shot a rabbit now and then, and maybe some squirrels. But the women hunted. My momma did.

"And so did I. I could hit a squirrel out of a tall tree."

Annie remembered it. It came back to her while she talked. She relived the story step by step.

"What the Yankees didn't know was we had guns. We had guns all over the place. You had to have a gun to eat. And you had knives for cooking with. We had these things, you see.

"When these widow women had enough of putting up with these soldiers, these three, they got together and talked it over. My mother was one of them. What I believe is the Yankees had forced themselves on some of these widows. They weren't old widows, you understand. These were war widows. And their brothers were gone, too, off in prison or dead in the war.

"The women got out the guns they had hid, and they sneaked onto Cedar Cliff that night. I went along, too, me and my momma did. I was young, and I could climb good. A gun is a heavy thing to carry up a mountain. Any ol' gun was heavy back then.

"There were five of us together that walked up Cedar Cliff that night. The Yankees had their horses tied in the trees. The horses didn't mind us one little bit. They just opened their eyes and watched us come right on by.

"The soldiers had a tent pitched on Cedar Cliff, but they weren't in it. That's where they kept the things they took from us. The Yankees were asleep out front on blankets on the ground."

The professor from the university scribbled away with his pencil, writing it all down. But Annie wasn't telling it to him anymore. She was telling it to herself. Out loud.

"We stood over them real quick," she said. "It didn't take any time at all. Now, I didn't hate those men as bad as my momma did. But I knew why we had come up there, and I knew what my job was. I sure did. We put our guns to their heads and fired all at the same time. The horses gave a snort and a holler when the guns went off. Those three Yankees were already dead."

Annie stopped talking. She'd been so scared that night that she was scared now to remember it. She opened her eyes and watched a breeze move through the trees. The tips of the pine needles glimmered in the sun.

"This must not sound like a story about dogs, does it?" Annie kind of laughed. There was more to tell.

The women hadn't known what to do next. They'd carried out their plan. Now, there were three bodies on the ground. They were afraid to leave them there. They were afraid they'd be caught and hanged, or that they'd have to leave their homes and hide out the rest of their lives over on the Tennessee side.

"We were home folks," Annie said. "We weren't renegades. We took the guns home and hid them away. Then the five of us came back with shovels. You couldn't get a wagon up Cedar Cliff. We untied the horses and ran them off. Somebody nearby would end up with them.

"We tried to dig graves for the men. One of the widows got very angry. She started crying and took her knife to one of the Yankees. She cut him up pretty good. Then she spit on him and cussed. My momma and me didn't think that was any way to treat the dead. No good would come of it, but we didn't say anything.

"You can't dig on Cedar Cliff. It's all rock up there. But we got the ground scooped out some. It was a miserable burial. We just couldn't get the hole deep enough for all three of those men. We scraped around with those shovels all morning and finally managed it. Then we carried rocks and stacked them over the grave. We spread the rocks around. You wouldn't know it was a grave if you saw it.

"The widow with the knife, I won't say which one, stopped crying when the job was done. She was the first one to see the dogs. These weren't regular dogs like you keep down to the house. These were big, black dogs. They were sleek looking. There was one for each of us. They followed us down from Cedar Cliff, and it was clear we could never go back to the place.

"They weren't normal dogs. They were larger than most dogs you see. And they didn't bark. They got in front of you and chased you. They jumped right in front of you. They were all black with big, red mouths, and they didn't make a sound but maybe for their breathing. Those dogs came up from hell when we buried those Yankees. The dogs wouldn't let us come back. They guarded the place to keep us away for good, or until we died, whichever came first."

Annie relaxed some. The story was over. She unknotted her hands and stretched her back a little.

"Those five black dogs haunted Cedar Cliff from that day on," she said. "I haven't been up there, but people say these days, there's only one dog left. I believe them, I sure do. Guess I was twelve at the time, maybe thirteen. Now, there's one dog left. He's the devil. He's waiting on me, you see. I reckon I won't be going to heaven.

"When I die, that dog on Cedar Cliff will be gone. He's the last one."

Pepper

Dinwiddie, Virginia

Pepper, a miniature version of a Scottish Terrier, was born with the disposition of a cat.

The pampered pet of Elizabeth MacLeod Warren, Pepper was aloof and petulant. Only his owner was allowed to pick him up or scratch his fur. And only she merited the little dog's complete attention. Otherwise, Pepper was perfectly capable of ignoring the close company of humans.

Pepper was especially content to ignore the presence of men in general and, later, Elizabeth's Virginian husband in particular.

Elizabeth was the younger daughter of Roderick MacLeod of New York. When she was sixteen, during the years of Prohibition, Elizabeth was sent on a tour of her family's homeland. She traveled to Scotland at her grandfather's expense. It was tradition that each of the MacLeod sons and daughters was brought to Dunvegan Castle on the Isle of Skye, where cousins still occupied the ancient ancestral home.

Tall and elegant, Elizabeth proved a favorite of the Dunvegan MacLeods. They took great pleasure in welcoming her to the family home and introducing Elizabeth to the wealth of history housed at Dunvegan Castle. They told Elizabeth numerous stories associated with the MacLeod clan. The family legends covered the full spectrum of Scottish lore and included Royal battles, personal tragedies, murders most foul, and, above all, great loves.

A black bull's head is prominently depicted at the top center of the MacLeod family crest. Elizabeth learned why.

Malcolm, the third chief of the clan, born in 1296, carried on a clandestine affair with the wife of Frasier of Glenelg. Upon leaving an assignation with his secret lover, Malcolm was confronted by a mad bull in Glenelg. Armed with only a knife, he battled the deranged beast. In the strenuous effort to save his life, Malcolm proved successful. The huge beast would not give up the attack until fatally wounded. As a souvenir of his prowess as a bull slayer, and perhaps as a lover, Malcolm retained one of the animal's horns.

Elizabeth was shown the horn, which is still on display in Dunvegan Castle today. It was a great clan treasure, she was told. Each male heir since Malcolm's battle with the mad bull has had to prove his manhood by draining this horn filled with claret.

Inside the stone castle, surrounded by sea mist come up from the rocky shore, Elizabeth listened intently to the family story of the fairy flag, the sacred banner that is said to possess miraculous powers for the MacLeod clan.

Many generations ago, when the handsome chief of Clan MacLeod came of age, he could find no young lady in the area who suited his fancy, although many were attracted to him. One day, in the far garden of Dunvegan Castle, he happened upon a fairy princess. She was one of the Shining Folk, who are known throughout Scotland.

Like all the other females he met, the fairy princess fell madly in love with him. Only this time, he fell madly in love with her as well. It is difficult not to love a fairy.

The princess soon asked permission of the king of the Shining Folk to marry the exceedingly handsome Laird MacLeod. The king refused, of course, saying that it would only break her heart to marry a human. Humans soon age and die. The Shining Folk live forever.

The fairy princess wept bitterly and seemingly without end. So relentless was her sorrow that the king eventually relented. He agreed that she and MacLeod could be married for a year and a day. At the end of that time, however, she must return to the Shining Folk. The fairy princess agreed to his stipulation. She and Laird MacLeod were married with great ceremony.

No happier time ever existed before or since for Clan MacLeod. The two were enraptured of each other. As might be anticipated, a strapping and handsome son was born to the happy couple before the year was out. The celebration went on for days.

The remaining time of the fairy's agreement passed very quickly. A year and a day were gone in a wink. At that time, the king of the Shining Folk came down from the sea clouds to the end of the great causeway of Dunvegan Castle. He waited there for Lady MacLeod to keep her promise.

The fairy princess held her son to her breast, hugging him tightly. It was impossible to say goodbye, but even more impossible that she should stay. She made her husband promise that her son would never be left alone, and that he would never be allowed to cry, for she could not bear the sound. At last, she fled the castle tower to meet the king of the Shining Folk and return with him to the land of fairies.

The handsome father kept his promise. Never was the young MacLeod allowed to cry, and never was he left unattended. However, Laird MacLeod remained deeply depressed and grieved for the loss of his love.

The folk of the clan decided that something must be done. On his birthday, a feast was held with great revelry and fancy dancing until dawn. The laird had always been a grand stepper. As the night wore on, he finally agreed to attend the festivities in his honor to dance to the pipers' tunes.

So great was the exultation upon the arrival of Laird MacLeod to his birthday celebration that the nanny assigned to watch the infant laird was overcome with curiosity. She left the nursery to see for herself what all the fuss was about. She came to the top of the stairs and looked upon the whirling folk in their finery and listened to the joyful music. She did not hear the infant laird awaken. The young maid did not hear him begin to cry.

His mother did.

She heard it all the way in the land of the Shining Folk. The beautiful princess, now a fairy again, immediately appeared at his crib. She took her baby son in her arms to comfort him. She dried his tears and wrapped him in her fairy shawl. She whispered magic words in the infant's ears, words that only fairies know, and lay her now-sleeping son back in his crib. She kissed him once and was gone.

Upon discovering the fairy shawl in the baby's crib, Laird MacLeod recognized it immediately. He knew that his former wife had been there and that the shawl was a magic talisman.

"Dare not touch the shawl," he warned the castle maids.

It was to be kept in a safe place.

"If ever the infant cries and cannot be made to cease his sorrow, summon me at once, and I will bring it to him."

The infant became a man, and the shawl became the MacLeod fairy flag. If ever the clan faced mortal danger, the flag was to be waved three times, and the hosts of Shining Folk would come to their aid. If anyone not of Clan MacLeod touched it, they would vanish in a puff of smoke.

There were to be few such blessings, Elizabeth was told

when she was shown the flag. They were to be used only under the direst of circumstances.

The new Laird MacLeod, upon reaching adulthood, placed the fairy flag in a special locked box. He carried it with him wherever he went, just as his fairy mother carried his memory in her heart wherever she went and for as long as she lived, which was forever.

Hundreds of years later, the fierce Clan Donald besieged the MacLeods in battle. The MacLeods were outnumbered three to one. Just before the last charge of the Donalds, the current chief of the MacLeods removed the fairy flag from its box. He secured it to a pole and waved it once, twice, and three times. As the third wave was completed, the fairy flag caused the MacLeods to appear to be ten times their number. Where there stood one MacLeod, the Donalds saw ten standing. Thinking that the MacLeods had been reinforced, the Donalds turned and ran. Clan Donald never threatened the MacLeods again.

On another occasion, a terrible plague killed nearly all the MacLeods' cattle. The clan chief faced the prospect of a winter of starvation for all his people. Having no alternative, he climbed the tallest tower of Dunvegan Castle, attached the fairy flag to a pole, and waved it once, twice, and three times. The Knights of the Fairie Raide, as they are known in Scotland, came down from the clouds, swords drawn, and rode like the wind over the dead and dying cattle. They touched each cow with their shimmering swords. Where once there had been dead and dying cows, there now stood healthy, fat cattle, more than enough to feed the clan for the winter.

The flag was brought from its box, and she was allowed to touch it. Elizabeth did not vanish in a puff of smoke.

If there are fairy shawls and fairy princesses, Elizabeth thought, *perhaps there are fairy princes, too.*

She spent the next day touring the castle gardens. Elizabeth explored the formal round garden, laid out in the 1700s, where she admired the many varieties of rhododendrons. No fairy prince she could see was hiding there. She followed winding paths through woodland glades, past shimmering pools of water. Alone, the sixteen-year-old strolled aimlessly along a brook fed by a cascading waterfall. She found no fairy prince, although she looked high in the branches of every tree. She'd have to marry a human, she supposed.

On Elizabeth's leisurely return to the castle, a woman appeared on the path. It was an old woman in a black dress and a blue bonnet, who approached from the direction of the castle. Elizabeth greeted her pleasantly in passing. The old woman did not reply. She never so much as looked at Elizabeth. She walked right on by.

On the night before Elizabeth's departure from Dunvegan, the fabled bull's horn was produced and filled to the brim with wine, which was then poured into a beaker. The beaker was offered to Elizabeth. Would she care to test her mettle as a true MacLeod?

Unaccustomed to alcohol, Elizabeth sipped the wine.

Before going to bed, Elizabeth told her hosts of the encounter with the old woman on the woodland path.

"What was she wearing?"

"A black dress," Elizabeth said. "A long, black dress."

"And was she sporting a blue bonnet?" a cousin asked.

Elizabeth said that she was.

"She wouldn't even look at me," Elizabeth said.

"That was the widow witch of Skye," the cousin told Elizabeth. "And look at you she did, I'll bet!"

Elizabeth had never before seen a witch.

The witch of Skye was one of the haunts of Dunvegan, Elizabeth learned as she sipped more wine. She had birthed seven sons by seven men in her life. Each son was born with a different last name. Each of the fathers died before the widow had another son by yet another husband.

Elizabeth was told the last names of the first six sons, all of whom had wed and raised families of their own.

"All the fair women of Scotland knew to avoid marrying the son of the blue-bonnet hag," Elizabeth's cousin said with a wink. "She sailed to America with her seventh son to find him a wife on that continent."

The widow witch had no luck. She was old by then and no one remembers, or perhaps no one ever knew, the last name of the last son.

"Aye, the heathen hag returns to Skye to choose among the fairest women of the world," Elizabeth's uncle said. "Only single women of marrying age see the witch. Be pleased she didn't speak to you, or you might have been introduced to her unwed son."

Elizabeth finished as much of the wine as she could manage and went directly to bed. She would be leaving early in the morning for her return to America. Everything she'd be taking with her was packed, except for the clothes she would wear. Or so Elizabeth believed.

The young American fell fast asleep. Elizabeth slept late into the night, when she was startled awake from fitful dreams of a fairy princess and the baby she left behind. The castle hounds were baying madly, as if beset by demons. But it was not the sound of dogs in the night that troubled her. It was the tall man sitting on the edge of her bed.

Elizabeth gasped. She thought to scream and almost did. Except that the man sat so quietly, without menacing her in any way, she would have screamed. The moment of terror quickly passed. He smiled kindly upon her, as Elizabeth would remember clearly. His eyes were bright, but she would not recall the color of them. He seemed handsome. She thought he might have been a prince. The man took her hand in his and cradled it gently, warmly. Elizabeth was not afraid. She waited for him to speak. He smiled once more and then was gone. Her hand was empty.

A little bedazzled, a little dazed, Elizabeth rose from her bed. The door to her chamber was locked. He had not come in that way. Elizabeth moved to the window. Had he come inside her room upon the sea mist? Outside, the night was dark and glum. There were no stars. The fog had moved in. The hounds continued their racket.

Elizabeth drew the curtains closed and returned to the bedside. There, she saw a pair of gloves where the man had been sitting. She saw them as plainly as if the room were flooded with sunlight. Elizabeth picked them up. They were lambskin gloves with long fingers and wide cuffs. Upon the cuffs was embroidered an intricate design in blue thread. Her visitor must have removed his gloves to take her hand in his.

She lifted the kid gloves to her cheek to make certain they were real. The soft leather caressed her skin. Then she looked more closely at the embroidery. She studied it as best she could. The decoration was clearly a monogram. But Elizabeth could not make out the letters, so fancy was the design. She traced her fingertips over the expertly knotted pattern of blue thread. It tickled her fingers. Still, she was unable to discern the lettering. Was it the monogram of a prince?

Carefully setting the gloves aside on a chair, Elizabeth slipped into bed. She was soundly asleep before the castle hounds ceased their mournful baying.

When she awoke in the morning, the gloves were gone. They were not on or under the chair. She looked for them everywhere, seeking proof her midnight visitor had been more than a dream.

Downstairs, before she had the opportunity to mention the man in her room, to ask if anyone had found a pair of men's gloves with blue embroidery on the cuffs, Elizabeth was shown a new excitement. She was handed a wicker basket not much larger than a purse, in which sat a darling, little puppy in black fur.

"We chose him small, so he might travel more easily on your journey home, Elizabeth."

Surely, puppies came no smaller than this one! She cradled him in her hands, lifting him to her face. His tufted ears tickled her chin. Elizabeth fell instantly in love.

"I'll hide him in my pocket, if I have to," she said.

＊＊＊＊＊

Back in New York, Elizabeth was courted by a steady stream of suitors. Pepper, of course, liked none of them. But Elizabeth liked one very much. A charming and responsible young man from Virginia stole her heart away. He was studying law. Upon his graduation, the young couple was wed. With her father's blessing, Elizabeth MacLeod married Kenneth Warren. Pepper followed at Elizabeth's heel as the radiant young woman, on the arm of her proud father, walked down the aisle in her bridal veil. The bride's only regret was that the groom's mother, at home in Virginia, was too ill to travel to attend the wedding.

The newlyweds took a fashionable apartment in the city. Pepper stayed mostly under the furniture whenever Kenneth was in the room. This was fine with Kenneth. He liked animals well enough. He just didn't see the need for having one indoors. He would never say a word about it to his wife, however. She was devoted to the little critter. Accepting Elizabeth's devotion to her dog, Kenneth decided, was a fair compromise of marriage.

Elizabeth soon had her own compromise to make. Word came that his mother had died, Kenneth said. He informed her he must travel quickly to Virginia to settle the estate. Elizabeth decided to make the trip with him.

"Is there a house where we can stay?"

"Perhaps the largest house in Dinwiddie County," he told her without boasting. "But it is in bad repair."

"I'd like to see it," Elizabeth said.

And so she did. Pepper came along.

The house of her husband's inheritance was in actuality a mansion, done entirely in brick and stone. Situated in a wooded area at the end of a long private drive shaded by stately pines, the home was far away from any neighbor. The acreage of the Warren estate numbered in the hundreds. It reminded Elizabeth of Dunvegan Castle, and she fell in love with the place.

Elizabeth had long dreamed of having her own small estate, complete with wooded paths and a variety of rhododendrons.

"We must live here," she said. "I'll design the gardens."

The gardens were Elizabeth's best prospect. The expansive three-story mansion was in such a dilapidated condition that she found it difficult to believe it had been recently lived in.

Kenneth wasn't sure he wanted to stay.

"We must," Elizabeth insisted. "We can restore one room at a time. It will be well worth the doing, my darling. You can practice law in Petersburg. Oh, please say we can keep it. Please!"

"I suppose I'm used to the place," Kenneth finally said. He had lived there a very long time before moving to New York to study law.

Soon, the roof was repaired. Workmen were hired to replaster the ceilings and walls. Elizabeth picked out wallpaper and rugs. She ordered furniture from catalogs. She worked endlessly on the gardens.

Pepper never left the house unless it was with Elizabeth, and he always stayed very near to her. He never chased rabbits or chipmunks and seemed happiest when Elizabeth went back inside.

Elizabeth and Kenneth were happy. Their love for each other didn't fade during their first few years in the new home. Elizabeth had only two regrets. One was that she wasn't pregnant yet. A room had been set side for the nursery. The other regret was that Pepper had not warmed to Kenneth's presence. Not one bit. The little black dog never reacted in any way to Kenneth's voice. He never came when Kenneth called. He never accepted food from Kenneth's hand. Except for hiding under the furniture in whatever room Elizabeth happened to be whenever Kenneth was home, Pepper seemed to pretend that her husband didn't exist. Elizabeth didn't quite understand it.

But there was another, larger thing that Elizabeth didn't understand.

The three-story back wall of the home was entirely covered in leafy vines when Elizabeth first saw it. She pruned away those that threatened to cover the windows on the first floor and chopped at the vines from inside open windows on the floors above. Four years after moving in, with most of the interior remodeled, Elizabeth decided the time had come to take down the vines entirely.

It was arduous work. Elizabeth, with Pepper at her side, would manage it piece by piece, first chopping the thick vines at the root. She accomplished little the first day.

Kenneth, when he came home in the late afternoon, found his wife chopping and tugging at vines at the back of the house. Pepper didn't even notice when he arrived.

"Perhaps the vines should stay," Kenneth said over dinner. "I can hire someone to trim the windows free each season and to prune the vines from the eaves where they're pulling down the guttering."

"I'll get it done," Elizabeth told him. It was her home now, and she was determined. "I'm a MacLeod, you know. And MacLeods know how to get things done."

Kenneth didn't argue with his wife, but he deeply wished she wouldn't remove the vines.

The next day, Elizabeth whacked away the leaves from the large vines she'd chopped off at the root the day before. Pepper was happy to attend the cutting of the vines. He studied his mistress at her work. Elizabeth paused from time to time to scratch his ears and ask him what he thought of her progress.

She tugged at the small vines from the main stalk where they climbed over the wall stones and tightly clung. There were vines upon vines, extending as much as three feet deep from the wall in some places. Her arms covered with scratches, Elizabeth pruned the vines as they grudgingly came free from their hold on her house. The pile of discarded vines grew behind her into a small mountain, although she had cleared but a small portion of the back wall of the house.

Elizabeth wiped her forehead with the back of her arm and began trimming at the next thickness of vines with garden shears. She saw something poking out at her from the vines. It looked like a crooked white finger.

"What can this be?" she said aloud, quickly cutting away more of the leafy tendrils.

Then she screamed, stepping back from her work.

Pepper barked at the vines and what stood hidden behind them. Elizabeth's heart raced with horror. There was an entire human skeleton standing in the vines. The white bones of a hand and an arm and ribs were trapped there, as if someone had been buried standing up against the wall. Buried in vines. Vines laced in and out of the openings of a human skull.

Elizabeth ran. Pepper stayed at her side, still barking. Stumbling in terror, Elizabeth circled the mansion and rushed inside the front door to await her husband's arrival. She was suddenly afraid of her own house. She was afraid as well of going back outdoors. She sat in a chair and waited, her eyes locked open in fear and wonder.

"There are bones outside!" she shouted at her husband the instant he was home. "There are bones!"

Pepper dashed under the sofa.

Kenneth Warren cocked his head to one side, trying to understand. He tried to smile at his wife, but it was not the time.

"A skeleton," Elizabeth stammered. "An entire human skeleton . . . I found it . . . I found it in the vines."

Kenneth held out his hand to his wife. He knew about the skeleton. He didn't know what he could say that Elizabeth would understand. His heart was breaking, and no words would come forth. He stood with his hand held out in front of him, as silent as a door.

"Whose are they?" Elizabeth asked, speaking rapidly. "Has there been a murder? Whose bones could they be?"

Her husband stood mute, his face washed pale as it drained of blood. It was clear to Elizabeth that he knew something he couldn't say.

"Kenneth!" Elizabeth demanded. "Tell me!"

"The bones," he finally said, "are mine."

He spoke so softly that Elizabeth wasn't sure she heard him speak at all. His mouth barely moved, but she understood the words as clearly as if they had been her own thoughts.

Kenneth disappeared. He went through the door without opening it. Or perhaps he vanished in thin air before her eyes.

Elizabeth fainted. Pepper rushed out from under the sofa and sat primly by her head upon the rug. When she came to, it was Pepper's bright eyes she saw. The little dog's being there saved her sanity, Elizabeth believed.

She locked the front door and climbed the stairs to her bedroom. She was exhausted and without appetite.

When she entered the room, Elizabeth immediately saw them on the bed. A pair of lambskin gloves with wide cuffs. Pepper leapt to the bed and took one in his mouth. Growling, he shook it viciously from side to side, testing to see if the white glove were alive. Elizabeth picked up the other one. Her husband's initials were embroidered in blue thread on the cuff.

It was her last night in the house.

The next day, she spoke to her neighbors. Everyone she

talked to was puzzled when Elizabeth asked about Kenneth's mother. They said that no one had lived in the house before Elizabeth and her husband moved in. No one had lived in the house for a hundred years or more.

In Petersburg, she learned that no one there had heard of a lawyer named Warren. Her husband's office did not exist. Elizabeth spoke to the sheriff about the skeleton and told him how to get in touch with her if it was needed. She left that day for New York with Pepper, leaving everything else in the house behind.

It was determined that the skeleton was at a minimum several generations old. Had a crime taken place, no one living could have been involved. The remains were buried in the public cemetery in an unmarked grave.

It is unknown whether Elizabeth MacLeod Warren married again. Perhaps when you marry a ghost, whether it be for a few years or a lifetime, once is enough.

One thing's for certain. If dogs could talk, Pepper would have told Elizabeth that no one real was ever there for four years of marriage.

Big Pigeon

Tobes Creek, Tennessee

Tobes Creek rushes down from Turkey Knob Gap in the Smoky Mountains to join the Big Pigeon a few miles inside the state line of Tennessee. The rocky landscape is shot through with caves among the steep rises and deep, green mountain ravines. It's not a place to have a farm of any kind. Swift, clean creeks are plentiful, especially when it rains, and there are enough tall spruces and firs that the air always smells sweet. The towering forest pines are undershot with stands of glossy-leafed rhododendron and mountain laurel trees.

The woods around Tobes Creek are full of snakes, butterflies, birds, and bees. And more than a few bears, most likely.

But only one or two families lived there.

Enzor Barshia did. He lived on Tobes Creek long before the Big Pigeon River got its name. Enzor called it "the river," that was all. He was afraid of it. And he was afraid of the rain.

Motorists who take Exit 451 off Highway 40 at Browns, Tennessee, can drive up Tobes Creek Road today and get lost on the forest trails where Enzor lived in his time. It's always been a private place. Young couples from the area, high-school kids and such, know where you can park at night. If you don't mind Hamblen crashing through the trees in the dark or scratching the paint on your car, you can have a fine time.

Hamblen was a "sanger." A sanger is a dog that can find ginseng growing in the woods. It's a valuable herb that grows wild in the high mountains of Tennessee. The people who live in these mountains call it "sang." Sanging was one of the few ways Enzor had of making any money at all.

Being a Beagle, Hamblen was a singer, too. He'd chortle when he ran. He'd howl when he stood still. And all the time, running or sitting, Hamblen would bark. That's what Beagles are for. That and flopping their long ears around. The fur on Hamblen's ears felt like silk. Enzor's mother said it felt like velvet. She'd owned velvet. She had a whole dress made out of it. She'd never owned silk.

Enzor Barshia was himself a curious breed, having been born a lazy man who couldn't sit still. It was almost a curse being born that way.

They say you can find God in the mountains without having to work at it much. That's what Enzor did. He found God on the bottom of a cave. Hamblen went along just because Enzor so rarely went anywhere. The cave was high above the river and high above Tobes Creek, yet there were fish-bone fossils covering its floor. They were more than bones. You could see where their eyes and mouths were, raised up from the rock foundation of the cave as if the whole fish were lying at your feet.

This puzzled Enzor. How the fish got there was a riddle. Being a lazy man, he liked riddles. He could sit with his foot tapping and puzzle over a riddle for days, which is what he did.

"It's the work of God," he told his dog one day.

Enzor had a revelation from seeing those fish fossils in a cave high on the ridge, high above the creek and river both, high above his cabin home. It was a vision that no one but Enzor could understand.

He tapped his foot and took to whittling on some wood he had. Enzor had a plan. It was right there in the Bible. Enzor's vision was a dangerous one. A lazy man with a plan can be a dangerous thing. He decided to try it out on his dog first, to see if he could make it work. Dogs, after all, are too dumb to help themselves.

"If there be an easier way to escape the flood, I don't know what it is," he said.

Noah had built the Ark, but an ark wouldn't do. Not in the mountains when the real flood came. A boat would get trapped in the trees. It would be broken against the rocks. There weren't any floods in the mountains that were gentle ones. You just couldn't get a boat to go. You might as well try to swim.

Enzor whittled on a piece of wood and then got tired. Being restless, he had to keep his foot tapping all the time. When he went to bed at night, his foot would keep tapping even in his sleep. His foot stayed wide awake while the rest of Enzor went to sleep. Because of this, he woke up tired almost every day.

"Enzor," his mother told him, "I don't know how we're supposed to tell when you're dead. Your heart will stop beating and your brains will fall out long before that foot stops going up and down."

He was her oldest son, and his mother thought Enzor might be crazy. So he wouldn't tell her anything. His vision required his finest concentration. Enzor somehow learned to move the tapping in his foot to his whittling hand. Things went faster after that.

He carved out a little model that had a place in the middle for his dog. It looked just like a boat to Enzor, with flat handholds on the sides. Only the handholds were for holding something else.

"Looks like a coffin to me," his mother said. "If you carve a lid for that thing, you can sleep outdoors from here on. It'll mean you're a witch."

It looked like a boat because he hadn't gotten around to making the wings yet. But Enzor didn't tell his mother a thing.

"Your dog is in the woods hollering, Enzor. Doesn't that mean something to you?"

Hamblen had found some sang. Enzor should be out there to mark the spot, his mother thought, if her son was good for anything.

"Means it's going to rain," Enzor said.

"It always does," his mother said. She had a broom in her hand. "It's always going to rain."

"That's what I mean. If not now, later."

Enzor took up more room than any two other people did. He would sit by the window when it rained with his legs sprawled out and his foot tapping along. When she was sweeping, his mother would try her best to get him to move. And since he was whittling on things the whole day, why, she was sweeping nearly all the time.

"Go outside," she said, "if you're going to be carving on that log. Take it outdoors with you."

Enzor wouldn't go outside when it rained, even though they had a roof over the porch, where he could sit without getting wet.

Enzor didn't talk much. He just sat there piddling with that thing. Sometimes, he would ask his mother for a drink of water. She always went to the well and retrieved him a drink when he asked for it, and Enzor always just swallowed it down. Sometimes, after he took a drink, he would say he was tired. Having a vision is a tiring thing.

The roof leaked. It wasn't a big spot, but enough that his mother had to put a pan under the leak to catch the rain. Whenever she said anything about splitting a few boards to patch it with, Enzor argued that it wouldn't do any good. It would take more than a patch on the roof to save them from the rain. Hamblen drank out of the pan. The tips of his ears got wet.

Enzor worked as fast as he could. He made a bigger model this time. It looked like a boat to him, with a place in the middle for his dog.

"You make one of those my size, and I'm throwing you outside for good," his mother warned. "Some witch stuck a thorn in a doll's foot the day you were born, and she can just come get you and take you home. You can live with a witch, for all I care. You won't be living here, you start making one of those boxes for me."

Except for a warning now and then, she left Enzor alone. She'd never seen him work on one thing so hard in his life, though it scared her more than a little bit. Especially during the last two weeks, when he took down a cedar tree on his own. Enzor said it had to be cedar, and that was all he would say.

He pulled along on that cedar log with a handsaw until it was almost ready.

It had to have bones, he decided, but he didn't say anything. He carved the boat about dog-size this time and added bones to it, bones made of bent willow limbs that stuck out both sides. Enzor put Hamblen inside to get the size just right. The Beagle sat there like a good pup and looked all around like he was about to go somewhere.

Colored white, black, and tan, Hamblen weighed only about twenty pounds. He was a compact, nicely built dog, with muscled legs and a thick chest. The legs were for sanging. The chest was for singing. Whichever Hamblen was doing, he did with concentration and full intent.

Enzor made hinges out of hickory bark. And he put a pedal in his cedar box.

He practiced with Hamblen. Enzor taught the Beagle to stand on the pedal with his front legs, then get off and stand on it again. He practiced with Hamblen till he had it just right. Hamblen had a good old time.

When Hamblen worked the pedal, the willow-branch frames to either side would go up and down on their hickory-bark hinges—you know, like wings. And that was Enzor's vision, to make a boat that would fly. Because the real rain was coming soon, the one that would raise the river to the top of the caves high in the mountainside, where the fish-bone fossils were.

Now his mother knew Eznor was crazy for sure. But she didn't mind. At least he was doing something besides sitting in the house with his foot tapping. And if that wood box of his really was a coffin, it wasn't a bad idea to make one that could fly. As long as Enzor didn't carve one her size, she could live with it.

Besides, it was the flying boat that got Enzor married.

Old Booger Topes lived in the next cove over from Enzor's. He had three daughters who were related to practically everyone except Enzor who lived on Topes Creek. Enzor was too lazy to do any courting. But the fact that his father was a rambling man who had run off and wasn't from the area to begin with put him in a pretty spot. Namely, he was free to pay a call on Old Booger Topes and his daughters.

First, Enzor took the covers off the bed and wrapped them around the willow branches. They weren't good enough.

So he took along Hamblen and walked to Old Booger Topes's house. He didn't wash up first or anything. Booger Topes kept mules on his place. That's what made Enzor get married.

Booger Topes's three daughters were named Tellie, Tillie, and Maude. The old man was standing in the yard with a hoe when Enzor came along. Enzor said he would marry any one of his daughters Booger chose in turn for Booger's giving him two mule hides. Topes liked the idea but said he'd sold the hides when his mules died over the years. He tanned the hides, sure, but had traded away every one.

Enzor stood on his left foot and tapped his right. He told Booger Topes what he needed the mule hides for. Topes said he had a better idea. He had a stack of possum skins. Enzor decided that might do. The old man went inside the house and asked the daughters which one of them wanted to get married most.

Enzor came home with Tellie by the hand.

Tellie followed Enzor inside the cabin. He patted her head like she was a dog and felt her ears.

"Get your fingers off her face," his mother said, "and let me see my new daughter-in-law."

His mother was happy with the situation. Tellie could go to the well when Enzor needed water. His mother wouldn't have to.

"Where do I sleep, Mrs. Barshia?" Tellie asked, wanting to see her new bed. She wondered if the quilt she'd tied in a bundle and brought along would do.

"I'd sleep on the left, if I were you. His right side has a kick."

Enzor spent his honeymoon stretching possum skins over the willow-stick wings of his pedal-box. He sewed them in place with a big needle, just like a woman making a quilt. Tellie thought it was funny to see a man sew. She spent her time out on the porch watching Enzor and having laughing fits. When she laughed, Hamblen howled.

Enzor broke one of the wings by sewing the skins too tight and had to start over. He made new ones all around, stronger this time, with thicker hinges. By the time he was through, Tellie was fat with a baby in her belly. And it was starting to rain.

"You can hear the river filling up," Enzor told his wife when they went to bed that night.

"I guess so," Tellie said. "Can't you make your foot stop doing that even for a little while?"

The rain let up the next day, and there was a bit of blue sky over the Barshia cabin. When it rains in the mountains, the clouds cover the top of the hills, then swoop down on top of you whenever they feel like it.

The genius craftsman Enzor Barshia tied ropes to the cedar box with pedal-operated wings that went up and down, just like they were supposed to.

Hamblen hopped inside the box.

"Don't pick it up by the wings," Enzor told Tellie and his mother.

He showed them how to use the ropes for grips, then led the way through the woods to a rock ledge over Topes Creek.

"It's getting heavy," Tellie said.

They were about halfway there.

She told Enzor's mother she was putting her side down for a minute. Enzor right away came back on the trail he was leading them on to see what the holdup was.

"Can't you have that dog get out and walk?" Tellie asked her husband.

"He needs the practice," Enzor said, tapping his foot.

"He needs to ride in it when it's not sitting still to get the feel of it. Besides, it's not the dog that's heavy, it's you."

Enzor was referring to Tellie's being pregnant, and she supposed he was right. It wasn't the dog, it was the baby that made the carrying hard. She picked up her side, and Enzor's mother did hers, and off they went before the rain started in again.

It was pretty at the creek. Tall green ferns grew among the trees. And there were little orange mushrooms. Wildflowers bloomed in profusion, grabbing sunlight with their faces before the rain came back down from the hilltops. Tellie liked the sound the water made rushing over the rocks.

Enzor said that this time, the creek was going to fill the river up. It had happened before. It was going to happen again. It was the core glimmer of his blinding vision, the river filling up.

They positioned the cedar box at the edge of the ledge above the creek. He had the women of his family back well away from his wooden bird.

"I'll do the work from here," Enzor said.

He stood directly behind the box with animal-skin wings. He told Hamblen to pedal. Enzor tapped his right foot.

Hamblen looked neither left nor right, but straight ahead. He was ready to fly. He jumped forward with his front feet, then shifted his weight from front to back. The wings went up and down on their double-strength hickory-bark hinges, which worked so smoothly they barely squeaked.

Tellie held her breath. Enzor's mother thought he was going to kill that dog, but it really wasn't all that far to the creek, and Hamblen knew how to swim, if his legs weren't broken from the fall. Enzor's foot tapped. The wings went up and down, up and down.

Hamblen barked. The winged box Enzor made lifted straight up, then fell forward, nose down, on the wind. Hamblen worked the pedal, and the nose lifted. Soon, he was twenty feet in the sky and moving right along. He had to follow the creek to the river to keep away from the trees. Sometimes, the homemade box that flew would dip a little. Other times, it sailed right along, Hamblen's ears flapping in the breeze like two ends of a silk scarf. Or maybe velvet.

Enzor grinned like a possum. Tellie clapped her hands. She somehow knew she was supposed to. She clapped her hands and wouldn't stop. Enzor's mother thought her son was crazy, sure, but now she knew just how crazy he was.

Hamblen was out of sight, flying above the river, up toward Hartford, then to Newport. He loved flying. What Beagle wouldn't? He could see everything from up there. Men fishing on the river watched the strange bird go by, and it's been known as the Big Pigeon River ever since.

The dog loved flying so much he never came back. The wind usually followed the river or the creeks. When Hamblen was thirsty or hungry, he found places for the cedar box to fall. He learned to press the pedal down to keep the wings up until his landing was complete. He missed Enzor, and he liked to say hello to people sometimes.

Hamblen would land his plane with a scratching, bumping, tree-crashing sound. The cedar box never broke, and he always kept the wings up. Folks like to think Hamblen came to the end of his years aloft.

Couples who park in secluded spots along Tobes Creek

say the area is haunted by a ghost, one that comes crashing down from the trees, then runs over and scratches the car door till you drive off. The people who know how the Big Pigeon River came by its name roll down the window and toss out a few French fries or a bit of their fast-food hamburger.

Enzor Barshia was proud to have saved his Hamblen from the flood. You won't find any dog fossils on the bottom of the caves in eastern Tennessee. Now that he was married and about to be a father, he had his family to think about. Any one of the rains that came could be the big one. His right foot tapping when his whittling hand went still, Enzor started to work on a baby crib made from a cedar log he'd cut.

Children and women first. That's the way Enzor thought of rain. Once you saved the dog, that is.

Moss Dog

Barataria Bay, Louisiana

Although there is a Jean Lafitte National Historic Park and Preserve in New Orleans, it was Pierre Lafitte, Jean's brother, who operated the family enterprises from New Orleans. The pirate smuggler Jean Lafitte spent most of his time in Louisiana on and off his ships among the islands of Barataria Bay. North of the bay is the town of Lafitte, named for him.

A hero of the Battle of New Orleans during the War of 1812, Jean Lafitte is better known as a pirate than a war hero. His ships were responsible for bringing many people to America. Most of them were slaves he'd stolen from Spanish ships. When the United States government sent troops to arrest Jean Lafitte in Barataria Bay, he slipped away to Galveston, Texas, where he operated for a few years before disappearing from history altogether.

It is believed the pirate moved his fleet to Mexican waters off the Yucatan. Many people suspect Jean Lafitte retired to one of the Barataria islands. There is a grave in the area that is said to be his. On one of the smaller islands is the grave of his Chinese lover, Kai Rin Hsin. There is yet another, much smaller grave. It is unmarked except by a small mound of miniature wild roses.

Kai Rin Hsin lived with her family within an island community of Chinese shrimpers who worked the waters of Barataria Bay. Jean Lafitte brought the family to Louisiana as captives from a pirated ship around 1810. Kai Rin was fourteen years old. Lafitte watched her grow to maturity and fell in love with the shy, hardworking, and beautiful girl. Her complexion was said to resemble polished alabaster. Her mouth was full, and her dark eyes glistened with excitement and dreams. The girl's hair was pure black silk that shimmered like threads of light.

Her father called Kai Rin a perfect rose.

She was the reason the pirate returned to Barataria Bay in his later years. Jean Lafitte was described in his lifetime as being six feet tall, with a dark complexion, black hair, and hazel eyes. Kai Rin referred to him always as "the Old Man."

Lafitte lavished the girl's family with gifts. Her father managed the entire shrimping community and was amply rewarded as loads of fresh shrimp were shipped to Pierre Lafitte's operations in New Orleans. Jean Lafitte was so enamored of the young woman that he brought with him on his piratical forays a Chinese interpreter known solely as Fritz. It was a nickname Jean Lafitte made up for him. The interpreter's sole function on ship was to translate Jean's letters to Kai Rin and the young girl's letters to him. She wrote him often, as he requested. Perhaps Kai Rin did so to please her family. Perhaps she was in love with the Old Man. All we know for certain of the letters is that Fritz copied them faithfully, lest he be butchered by the pirate and cast to sea.

At age sixteen, Kai Rin was no longer required to work the waters of Barataria Bay. Her primary function became that of serving as Lafitte's emissary among the members of her Chinese shrimping community. She also acted as a visiting nurse to individuals and families. The letters Lafitte sent to her included instructions he meant to have circulated among the Barataria Bay Chinese.

Kai Rin often visited a young woman, Kar Lee, who had been transported to the United States from Canton, where the Hsin family was from. On one such visit, Kai Rin learned that Kar Lee's little brother had suffered a serious injury. His sister was distraught. Nothing Kai Rin could think to say eased her best friend's anguish.

Kar Lee believed the injury to her brother would prove

fatal. A Chen had been bitten on the hand by a dog while picking wildflowers on one of the small, mossy islands of Barataria Bay.

"It was the Moss Dog," her friend told Kai Rin.

The Moss Dog was known to have teeth as sharp as thorns.

In an effort to save the youngster's life, Kar Lee's father amputated the boy's right hand. A boy's losing his right hand is a tragedy in a fishing family. A Chen would be unable to complete his apprenticeship to the trade. The entire family was overcome with gloom.

"He will die," his sister said. "He will die anyway. The curse will kill him."

In a few days, the boy was dead. Kai Rin wrote to Lafitte, telling him there was no reason Kar Lee's brother should have died. The hand amputation was clean and well tended. There was no infection. He died of fear. Kai Rin told him little of the Moss Dog.

Kai Rin's father had brought a small, silky dog hidden in his robe sleeves to America. He'd kept the dog alive through all the family's tribulations, but the miniature dog had not fared well on the small islands of Barataria Bay. He soon died and was buried.

Within the Chinese community of shrimpers, the rumor spread that her father's dog was a Moss Dog. Kai Rin would not believe this. The others were jealous of her father's position of authority on the islands. A Moss Dog is a ghost. Her father's dog was a Pekingese, a tiny, cuddly, pug-nosed pet. Though one was as small as the other, there was a world of difference between the two.

She knew where his dog was buried but would tell no one.

Lafitte wrote back to Kai Rin to instruct her father to have the dog that had bitten Kar Lee's brother found immediately and killed. He understood how cultural superstitions influenced a tightly knit community. Others would become convinced that they, too, were victims of the Moss Dog unless the animal was killed and its body shown to the Chinese shrimpers.

"I cannot find a ghost," her father complained. "Lafitte doesn't understand the situation. He believes the Moss Dog is real. That it is here on the islands. Write to him, Kai Rin, and inform him that the Moss Dog dwells only in our people's minds."

Kai Rin did so at once.

When Lafitte's reply finally arrived, he was adamant. Whatever dog it was that bit the boy must be found and killed. If there was a bite, there was a dog. Lafitte didn't care what it was called. He insisted that his instructions be carried out.

The story of the Moss Dog is an ancient one known throughout Asia. A daughter of a Chinese emperor was sent by sea with gifts for a distant king the emperor hoped to engage in trade. The princess of the Royal house had never set foot on earth and was carried in a Royal seat by her bodyguards. An ambassador of the emperor accompanied the princess on her voyage.

The princess wore a six-pound Pekingese in her sleeve. The dog's teeth had been filed to razor-sharp points. Its sole duty was to lash out at anyone who might dare attempt

223

to touch the Chinese princess. Though small, the dog was believed to be of the ancestry of a lion. Its body was big enough, barely, to hold a lion's ferocious heart, the beating of which pushed the little dog's eyes forward into rounded domes.

The voyage was ill-fated. A storm drove the ship into uncharted waters. It was carried by prevailing winds and ocean currents into new seas. Months passed, and all on board perished.

Eventually, the empty ship, its sails in tatters, drifted into waters crossed by pirates. A vessel of clandestine adventurers was quick to try to salvage the empty ship and take it over as one of their own. A cannon was fired across the empty ship's bow. Having met no resistance, no sign of life at all, the pirates pulled alongside the Chinese ship and tied to it.

Once aboard, they found more treasure than they'd hoped. Under an embroidered imperial tent was a large ivory box carved with mythical figures. The box was as large as a bed. It had a door held shut with a golden latch.

Upon finding booty on a conquered vessel, the captain of a pirate ship insists under penalty of death that no chest or box of any kind be opened unless he is present. The ivory box was brought on deck. Several men were required carry it. The golden latch was slashed by sword. The lid was lifted so all could see what was inside the ivory carriage.

The box was filled with the emperor's gifts of gold trinkets and jewels. It also housed a complete skeleton of human bones and a few smaller bones that looked as if they might be those of a rat. Whoever died in the ivory box had not experienced a pleasant death.

The first to reach his hand inside was inflicted with an intense pain, as if bitten by razors, and drew his hand back with a howl. It was a small bite that would not cease its bleeding until the man was dead. Another was ordered by the captain to retrieve the contents from the box. He suffered the same fate.

It was then that the woman appeared in Chinese robes of finest silk, robes that touched the ship's deck when she walked. The ghost of a female member of the Chinese Royal family has no feet. Her hair was untied, as if combed by rain. It hung loose over her shoulders like black silk threads.

She spoke softly, but all gathered on deck could hear and understand what she said. Ghosts speak the language of their listeners. She and she alone, she said, could reach into the ivory box without being bitten by the Moss Dog. She would be glad to retrieve the treasure for the pirate captain and his crew. She possessed no earthly interest in gold baubles set with jewels.

Her favor, which must first be met, was that she be delivered to her homeland aboard the pirates' ship. It would cost the pirates nothing but time. She required no cheese, no rum. A ghost does not eat or drink. She would sleep, she said, in the ivory box, which they had intended to carry on their ship in the first place.

Although many among the crew were superstitious of allowing a ghost on board their vessel, the captain agreed to her request. The carved box was transferred to their ship. A variety of plunder from the Chinese vessel was also brought aboard. It included a number of impressively etched Chinese swords. In far worse repair than she originally appeared, and unworthy of capture, the vacant ship was set afire and abandoned to the sea.

The captain had an advantage over the ghost. She did not know her location on the globe. Impatient to be rid of the ghost and to have his treasure, he brought her to landfall on the nearest shore in the dark of night and told her it was a southern bay of the Chinese continent. A dinghy was prepared to row her ashore. Two men were assigned the task. A Chinese ghost cannot cross water unless it attaches itself to a vessel. Many ghosts dwell at the bottom of the rivers of China.

The princess was excited to be home. But there was a problem. She could not leave the ivory box. She was tied to it in the afterlife. She and the captain devised a remedy. A small corner of the ornate box was broken off with a saber blow. It was no larger than an amulet. The princess wore the ivory around her neck and found that she was free to travel ashore.

The lid was lifted from the ivory box, and she placed the Moss Dog ghost into her sleeve. The dinghy was rowed to shore. The gold and jewels were emptied from the Chinese box, and it was smashed to bits by the pirate crew. The bones from inside the box were tossed into the ocean.

The captain raised sail and returned to the open sea, leaving his rowers on the dinghy to their own devices.

The princess's ghost was enraged to discover she could not step from the boat onto land. It was not China. Only the earth of China might receive her feet. She blinded the boatmen in her rage.

"Where am I?" she wailed. "Where have you brought me?"

"A new land," one sailor said. By being helpful, he might have his sight returned, he believed.

"It is owned by both the Spanish and the French," the other told her. "It is a new continent."

That is all the princess learned. Her bones scattered to the sea, she could not return to them. Not ever.

The princess took pity on her guardian dog. Life in a rowboat would be torment. She set it free by telling it to leap ashore. She flung it from her sleeve. Upon landing, the dog ran a little distance and then stopped. It dropped to the ground on its belly.

"It must be buried," the princess said.

"What can we do about that?" one of the rowers asked. "Neither of us can see."

"I'll describe the direction for your feet," the ghost told them. "Take your daggers and dig a grave. I will not let the Moss Dog bite you or harm you in any way."

The princess, sitting primly in her Royal silks, directed one of the rowers to his task. He felt for the little dog's body on his hands and knees where she told him to, and found it. He quickly dug a grave and placed the dog in it. Doing so, he felt a collar on the dog. He felt the jewels mounted on the collar. He'd come back for it, he decided. He marked the grave with a small trench on top, then crossed it with another.

When he rose from his work, the princess called to him

so he could find his way to the dinghy in the pure black darkness of the blind.

"This way," she said.

But the pirate wasn't going back. He'd had enough of ghosts. He tramped inland, his hands held out before him to find his way. He tumbled into a ditch and climbed out the other side. Eventually, he made his way to a path, a road, a town. He told a story to any who would listen, a story that nobody believed. He was arrested for piracy and died in prison.

Perhaps he was the lucky one. The other boatman rowed from shore upon the command of the princess, who meant to return to China. She promised him his sight back when they arrived. His own thoughts were silly ones, which helped him to avoid dying of terror from being in a small boat with a ghost. His own thoughts were that if he rowed hard enough in the general direction from which he came, he would come upon his mother ship and be rescued.

The princess's ghost is said to sit in the dinghy yet, commanding her blind companion to keep rowing. Lost at sea, they have been seen moving among the Caribbean islands, the boat rowing in circles. The dinghy has been spotted in the Gulf of Mexico at night and along the Florida coast in the middle of the day. Upon being hailed from a ship, the rower with the lady dressed in silk shouts, "Ahoy!" Then the small boat disappears and cannot be found. The woman in silk robes is always said to have long black hair draped loosely over her shoulders.

The cross made by a pirate's dagger upon the grave of

the Moss Dog remains. The ravages of weather have not removed the carved earth. Because of this, the grave itself can be identified, if found. It should not be disturbed.

That is the story of the Moss Dog, as everyone knows it.

Kai Rin thought of a way to satisfy Lafitte. If the Old Man wanted a dog's remains shown to the people of her fishing community, she would do that. As much as she loathed the prospect of disturbing a grave, digging up her father's dog would satisfy everyone, it seemed. She and her family could retain their status, both with Jean Lafitte and with the other Chinese families of Barataria Bay.

Having once known where her father's dog was buried, she thought she would be able to find the location right away. But it was not exactly where she remembered it. She searched two of the smallest islands without finding it. On the third, she had better luck. In a clearing where there was a gentle rise of land from the swamp, Kai Rin came upon the grave.

It had changed with the weathering of rain. Still, she recognized the partridge roses her father had planted in memory of his companion. These miniatures are one of the few roses known to grow to the edge of seawater. They are low, spreading roses with glossy, dark green foliage, from which spring clusters of dainty pink buds that open into perfect white blossoms.

Looking upon the roses, Kai Rin saw that they had formed themselves into a cross, as if trenches had been fashioned for their growth. She gasped and backed away.

Kai Rin studied the grave, walking around it. Maybe it was her imagination, she thought. The plant looked sort of like a cross, but it wasn't a cross really. It was the place her father had buried his pet, nothing more than that.

She'd brought along a trowel and a cloth sack. Kai Rin dropped to her knees next to the little mound of partridge roses and stuck the trowel into the earth. She must do this for her family. Her father would be removed from his position of authority by Jean Lafitte if she failed to produce the dog's remains.

She scratched the back of her hand on a rose thorn. It bled and would not stop. It was a tiny cut. She had not dug deeply in the earth at all, but the grave was disturbed. Kai Rin regained her feet and put her hand to her mouth. Her mouth filled with blood. She spit it out.

Her eyes widened in horror. Sitting on the grave was a silky dog with a pug nose and a feathery tail. It looked up at her with large, glimmering eyes. A collar of gold set with emeralds was around its neck.

Kai Rin shook her bleeding hand. Instead of thorns, the partridge roses had razor teeth. She could see that now, and she saw her end.

Jean Lafitte sailed to Barataria Bay at once upon hearing of her death. Her body was interred in a secluded spot on high ground. He said he wanted to be buried next to Kai Rin Hsin. When the time came, he would return.

Louisiana coastal fisherman will answer a tourist's question when asked.

"Moss Dog," one will say. "I know something about

that. It's a local name for a poisonous sea creature. Jellyfish, you know, pack a mighty sting."

"No," his companion will correct him. "It's a crawfish, he means."

They know better.

People with metal detectors still find old coins that wash ashore from shipwrecks along the Gulf coast, especially after storms sweep through the area. There's a pure-gold dog collar set with precious stones buried on one of the islands of Barataria Bay. It's waiting for someone unlucky enough to find it.

It's probably good advice not to pick any roses along the way.

The Whirlpool

Tiptonville, Tennessee

Ray Ross, Jr., lived with his skinny yellow dog, General George, in a sharecropper's shack on a small bayou just this side of the Mississippi River. The flat river country is known for its cotton. But Ray quit picking cotton years ago. He found a better way to make a living. He caught catfish in the Father of Waters. Big catfish. Catfish big as hogs. He sold them at the market in Tiptonville.

Ray had a little boat he kept in the willows by the river. He had a small wagon and owned a mule. He and General George, whose nose was always wet, would ride the wagon into Tiptonville twice a week with his catch. He kept the fish fresh in the little bayou alongside his shack until market day.

He played an old box guitar that had been his father's. Ray and General George would sit outside his shack of an evening and serenade the catfish. The fish liked being sung to. It kept their minds off of the predicament they were in. General George sang right along with Ray, howling when Ray sang the low notes, whining when Ray hit a high one. They knew all the catfish songs.

General George was no breed of dog to speak of. Skinny yellow dogs are not really all yellow. Some look a little orange, while others might seem sort of brown. Their hair is either short or long and can be smooth or rough, though usually somewhere in between. Skinny yellow dogs have a peculiar sideways gait when they come walking toward you. It looks like the front end is out of alignment, and they favor using one back leg at a time, resting the other in case of an emergency.

Famous for their nonchalance, skinny yellow dogs don't like to run. They just lope along. They've seen it all before. Skinny yellow dogs are often preoccupied with their thoughts. They stop whatever they're doing every now and then and stare off into the middle distance while they ponder a passing fancy.

Not really a breed at all, skinny yellow dogs are, though,

a definite type. They're born dreamers. And General George was one of those. This part of the country has had such dogs for longer than anyone can remember.

Ray had heard that dogs' noses are always wet because Noah used his two dogs to herd the other animals on to the Ark. They were the last aboard, by which time the Ark was crowded full. They had to ride out the forty-day flood with their noses stuck out in the rain. Ever since, dogs' noses are always wet.

General George's nose was always wet for another reason. He liked water. He'd jump in the river whenever he felt like it. And he always had his face in a puddle. If he had the desire, General George would be good at catching fish, Ray believed. If he could hold his breath long enough to go after one, that is.

Ray ran a couple of taut lines in the big river, lines tied with treble hooks and smell bait, just above Burrus Landing. This part of the Mississippi was once lined with cliffs, but the New Madrid earthquake of 1811 knocked them all down flat. It changed the course of the river.

The whirlpool in the river that General George always barked at was left over from the quake. It spun in a circle and never stopped. If you ever got caught in that whirlpool, you likely wouldn't get out. Ray had seen driftwood logs spin down under the water into the whirlpool and never come back up.

Mermaids came up the Mississippi River from New Orleans. That's what caused the earthquake. Mermaids like sailors, and they sing to them, trying to get them to jump into the water. They followed the boatmen up the Mississippi, singing the whole way. Trouble was, the water got shallow in one of the ribbon bends of the Mississippi, there along the Missouri boot heel. One of those mermaids got caught. Two fellows threw up a fence around the shallow hole she was in, trapping her on a sand bar.

In those days before the levees were built, the river shifted course as often as a child changes his mind, creating and taking away sand islands right and left. Sometimes, a little island would appear one day and be gone the next.

When you hold a mermaid captive at sea, it starts a hurricane. Everyone knows that. But there aren't any hurricanes in Tennessee. When those boys caught that mermaid in a fence, the earthquake started. It started in 1811 and didn't stop until 1812. It changed the course of the river, cutting off one big loop of the Mississippi right there at Tiptonville. Today, that part of the river is an eighteen-mile-long lake they call Reelfoot.

The earthquake brought the deep water over to where the mermaid was trapped. When she swam free, it stopped.

The only river mermaids left today live in little houses at the bottom of whirlpools. They don't come to the surface much, though you might hear one singing when a boat goes by late at night.

Ray ran his taut lines early in the morning. Mostly, those big catfish ate at night, and that's when the lines hooked them. If you waited too long, a big catfish would get off the hook and be gone with your bait. So it had to be early in the morning. General George rode in the little boat with Ray, barking at the herons and pelicans that flew overhead, sticking his nose in the water whenever Ray stopped to pull in one of the lines to see how big the fish was that was on it.

His catfish in the boat, Ray headed home. The big fish flopped around and groaned some under the wet burlap Ray had used to cover them up. He rowed his boat carefully around the whirlpool. General George barked at the deep swirls of muddy water.

Later, when Ray thought about it, he guessed he got the boat too close. General George jumped into the river, paddling hard to keep his head above water. Still barking, he was sucked into the whirlpool in no time flat. The skinny yellow dog spun in a circle once or twice, his ears floating on the surface, and then under he went.

Now, Ray couldn't swim too well when he had his clothes off. He couldn't swim at all with his boots on, or he might have jumped in after his dog. Besides, there was no telling how deep that whirlpool was.

He missed General George something awful. That's the way it is with skinny yellow dogs. You don't realize how much you love one of them until it's gone. Ray moped. He had the blues. He took his catfish to the market, but it wasn't fun anymore. He sat there by his bayou in the evening, his guitar in his lap, and didn't play a lick. Ray didn't feel like it. He didn't run his taut lines. He didn't bait a hook. Ray didn't want to go by the whirlpool again. He didn't want to see the place where General George went under. Ray didn't want to do much of anything.

Sunday, he didn't go to church. The pastor came by late in the afternoon, after he'd eaten lunch at somebody else's place, to check on Ray.

"I guess you could say I'm sick, pastor. I don't feel much like getting up."

"Heard about your dog, Ray," the pastor said. "The whirlpool in the river got him, was that it?"

"Yup. Took him under and wouldn't let go. General George is living at the bottom of the river now."

"That ain't no place for a dog, Ray."

The preacher looked off to one side. He cleared his throat. He tugged at his tie.

"A Christian man who's caught up with his tithing might find help from someone who knows the river."

Ray Ross, Jr., thought about it a minute. The preacher was right. Ray got a nickel out of the tobacco tin he kept under the porch of his shack and gave it to the preacher.

"Thank you, pastor," Ray said. "Thank you very much."

Ray combed his hair as soon as the preacher left and bounded out the door with a small sack of coffee beans.

Nobody knew more about the Mississippi River than Auntie Hodge did. She was older than the river, people said, with at least as many wrinkles. Auntie Hodge was a granny woman people went to when they needed to be cured of ailments and the like. She could whisper a splinter out of your foot, although it didn't always come out the same place it went in. She made warts go away by telling them to and wagging her finger at them.

237

He walked to her shack at the edge of the cypress trees on Reelfoot Lake. The path to her place wound through swamp timber woven thick with wild grape and other vines.

Ray offered her the sack of coffee beans as a gift and asked if she could help.

"Dogs chase cats, Mr. Ross," she said.

Auntie Hodge didn't have any teeth left, and you had to listen close to get the words right. One of her eyes sometimes looked in the wrong direction from the other one, making it hard to concentrate.

"Dogs chase cats," she said again. "That's what you have to remember."

"But he drowned in the river," Ray said. There weren't any cats.

"It was the whirlpool, you say? If that's so, then your dog didn't drown, Mr. Ross. Mermaid came up and got him."

"A mermaid did?"

"Now, here's what you got to do. You got to take your boat to the whirlpool at night."

"I don't know about that, Auntie Hodge."

"You got to," she said. Her eye drifted askance, then came back. "You take your shirt off, and you take a lantern. You stand by that lantern with your shirt off, so the mermaid can get a good look at you. They're lonely women, mermaids are. There aren't any mermen in the river, so they get lonely."

The mosquitoes will eat me alive, Ray thought.

"You take your guitar, and you play the best you know how. You got to serenade the mermaid, you see. You do that, and she'll come up and get you. You mark my word, Mr. Ross. You'll get your hound back, you will. If that's what you want."

It was a lot to do for a dog. But General George wasn't just any dog. He was Ray's.

"One more thing, Mr. Ross," Auntie Hodge said. "Don't forget to take your shoes off. A mermaid won't have a man come to her house unless he takes his shoes off first."

Ray hurried home. He got what he needed.

He carried his guitar and a lantern to the river. He pushed his boat into the water and sat down in it, waiting for it to get dark.

The frogs jumped into the river when the sun went down. There must have been a hundred of them. Night birds squawked. Bats flew out of the trees and chased insects out over the river. Fish leapt from the water and fell back in.

Ray was troubled. Lantern or no lantern, he didn't want to go anywhere near the whirlpool at night. And he didn't feel like singing. A man doesn't feel like singing to mermaids when he's got the blues.

He was sad about his dog. There was a big hole in his life. And that hole would be empty forever, Ray decided, if he didn't do something about it. Then he guessed he'd better hurry on up. He didn't know how long a dog could live underwater.

Soon, the night's water rolled under his rowboat, and Ray made steady progress toward the whirlpool. He poled to the shore and tied his boat to a tree limb. The whirlpool was just over there. Ray took his shirt off and picked up his guitar. The mosquitoes found him.

He tried strumming a song he knew and humming along. It came out deep and mellow. It came out sad instead of pretty. Auntie Hodge said it had to be a pretty song. But sad was all Ray could do.

"I never seen a pretty girl in all my life," he sang, "that she wasn't already somebody else's wife."

He looked to the whirlpool on this side of the Mississippi. Nothing but water was there. He played a little more, then sang a little louder.

"I went on board the other day,/Just to see what the boatman's wife would say./It was there I let my passion loose,/And now they got me in the calaboose."

The whirlpool spun empty as before. It wasn't the right song. Ray thought he might not know the right song anyway, so he began to cry. He couldn't help it. He kept playing his guitar, and he made it cry, too. He slid his fingers along the frets until the notes whined high and shivered low. His guitar wept.

Damn old dog anyway, he thought.

"When you go to the white man's ball,/Dance with the boatman's wife or not at all./I'll see you when they grab the noose/And throw you in the calaboose."

Ray wondered if the mermaid was dancing with General George. He smiled in a small way, just at the corners of his mouth. You let him, that skinny yellow dog would put his paws on your shoulders and walk you backwards across a room. Ray played a little faster, sang a little louder. He got some of the words to come out high. He kicked off his shoes. The boat rocked.

"Mermaid, mermaid," Ray sang. "Let your hair hang low./I'll give you more money than your lap will hold."

And there she was. The mermaid came up at the center of the whirlpool. She emerged from the churning swirl complete and whole, as if standing on the water. She glowed. She beckoned.

Ray set his guitar aside and, taking a big gulp of mosquitoes, leapt into the Mississippi River.

It's a big river, and he couldn't swim well. Ray managed to keep from drowning, by dog-paddling mostly, until he kicked his way to the edge of the whirlpool. The eddy grabbed him and pulled hard on the length of his body. The water pulled his pants off, and his underwear, too. He barely had his head above water.

The mermaid took him in her arms and told him her name. It was Becky. She wrapped Ray's face inside her long hair so he wouldn't drown, then swam to the bottom of the river with him held close to her body. Becky swam real well, Ray noticed. Then again, he figured, most mermaids probably did.

Becky lived in a house just like yours, except it was underwater. Ray could breathe just fine inside the house. The water didn't burn his eyes. He sat in a big stuffed chair and looked around. There were pictures on the wall. They looked like pictures of fish.

"That's my mother," Becky said, "when she was younger." When Becky talked, bubbles came out of her mouth.

The mermaid was happy to have company. She fixed Ray Ross, Jr., a fine meal of oysters and snails, served in a turtle bowl. There wasn't any cornbread. And there weren't any beans. You couldn't smoke even if you wanted to. For dessert, she gave him more oysters and snails.

"I guess I've had enough," Ray said. Bubbles came out of his mouth, too. "Maybe I better go."

Becky lay down on the couch and put her feet up. She wiggled her toes. Ray counted them. There were ten all told. Ocean mermaids have fins for legs, but river mermaids have feet just like real women do.

A crawfish shot through the living room and tucked itself backwards under a couch cushion.

"You'll like it here. I'll be a good wife to you."

"You mean we're getting married?"

"Same as," Becky said. "We already are. I've been married before, you know. I know the things I'm supposed to do."

Ray leaned back in the chair. He put his hands behind his head. He was getting used to living without clothes.

A river turtle walked upside down across the ceiling.

"I couldn't marry anyone," he said, "without that my dog came along, too."

"I have a dog," she said brightly.

"What kind of dog would that be?"

"Regular dog," Becky said. "A skinny yellow one."

Ray knew the dog she meant was General George. She'd stolen Ray's dog without knowing it was his.

"And where might he be?"

"He's busy now. He's a working dog."

Ray wondered about that. General George, a working dog? Why, there wasn't any work that dog would do.

"What kind of work does a mermaid need a dog for?"

"Chase away the catfish," Becky said. "This river is full of them."

Dogs chase cats! Of course, Ray thought. Auntie Hodge had told him to remember that.

"Why don't you sing me a song, and we'll go to bed," Becky said.

Ray counted the bubbles. There was one for each word.

"I'm mighty tired, and that's a fact. I'd like to go to bed real soon. But I can't sing a song without my guitar, and it's in the boat. Besides, that dog of yours was my dog first, and I came to get him back."

"I have a lute," Becky said. "I'll play that for you, and you can sing. I have a ship's bell, too."

"What about my dog?"

The mermaid stood up from the couch. She paced the floor of her underwater house, her hands on her hips. Ray watched her hair floating behind her head as she walked. It was as pretty as her toes.

"I can't let you have him," she said. "The catfish have gotten awfully bad. Without your dog, they come right into my house. They have those awful whiskers, and they knock things off the shelves with their tails. And I can't bear the racket they make at night, sifting through the beer cans at the bottom of the river."

"I'll catch them for you," Ray told her. He was happy

to be of help. "That's what I do. I fish them big cats. I'll move my lines to right by the whirlpool. I'll put more lines in the water. I'll use more bait. I'll catch those catfish for you, I promise."

"Are you sure you can?" Five bubbles lifted in line from her lips.

"Yes, ma'am. You ask anyone. I'm the best there is. Trouble is, I don't feel much like fishing unless I have my dog with me."

"All right then," the mermaid said. "You can go back and take your dog with you. Since you haven't kissed me yet, even though we're the same as married, you can go back up and you won't drown. If you want to kiss me, you'll have to stay."

This was a twist Ray hadn't expected. And it was a burden. He had been wanting to kiss Becky all along. But a skinny yellow dog, one that you've had for a long time and have gotten used to, is more important to a man than a mermaid. He guessed he'd never know how mermaids kissed, whether they were better at it than real women.

"I want my dog," he said.

Becky opened the door and called General George in. He ambled around the house like he didn't even care that Ray was there. But Ray knew better than that.

"There's one more condition," the mermaid said. "There's one more thing I want you to do."

She told him what it was, and Ray agreed to it.

"Once a week, then, unless I'm sick that day," he promised.

Minutes later, she brought Ray to the surface of the Mississippi River, his face wrapped in her long hair. His head bobbed in the water, the whirlpool pulling him back. The mermaid slipped down low and gave Ray a strong kick with both her feet. His body slid through the dark water. Ray didn't stop until he bumped into his boat. He climbed in. It was a strenuous effort. His pants were back on, and he didn't know how that could have happened.

He held the lantern over his head and watched the whirlpool. General George bobbed to the surface. She must have kicked him, too. The skinny yellow dog slid through the water like he had a motor tied behind, until his nose bumped the boat and Ray pulled him in. He untied the boat and rowed to his landing spot.

Every Saturday night after that, Ray Ross, Jr., came to the river's edge with his guitar, as he had agreed to do. He sang by the water's edge, playing his best songs. Someone was listening. General George howled and whined to almost every number, and sniffed the darkness when Ray was through.

As boatmen on the Mississippi guide their cargo at night around the whirlpool near Burrus Landing, they sometimes hear a dog howl. When they listen closely, they hear guitar music as well.

Ray Ross, Jr., died years ago. He's buried in Tiptonville. General George passed, too. Somebody else has a skinny yellow dog for a companion now. He should know to keep the dog from the river's edge. The catfish are stacking up down there.

Elf House

Gilmer County, Georgia

Disappointed in love, Stanwell Perpett came to the Appalachian foothills of northern Georgia to be alone for a while and to write novels. The locals say he came from New York City or Chicago. They don't know for sure. All they know is that he came alone and lived alone. Alone, that is, except for his dog.

Chaucer was a cream-colored dog, likely a White Shepherd and Golden Retriever mix. He had a friendly face. Like most mixed-breed dogs, Chaucer's ears got the worst of it. One white ear stood perfectly upright. The other flopped gently over at the tip. Whenever the dog approached his master, he lowered his head and wiggled his rear. It was Chaucer's dance of happiness. He had a tail that could knock over garbage cans.

Stanwell had been a successful attorney when his wife left him. He was taken by surprise by her doing this. In fact, Stanwell was stunned. They were too old, really, for her to be running off. Just past fifty, Stanwell had become solidly entrenched with the idea that he and she were companions for life. Not so, he guessed now. He filed for divorce on the grounds of abandonment. No one showed up in court to contest it. His wife didn't ask for and didn't receive a penny. The only thing she took with her was her freedom. He had his freedom as well, although he hadn't actually asked for it.

Suddenly a middle-aged bachelor with plenty of money in the bank, the attorney had a new perspective on life. A client of his from Georgia had spoken endlessly of the area in southern Gilmer County where he was from. It was at the edge of the Appalachian Mountains. The client spoke of whispering pines, of clear water tumbling over mountain rocks, of apple orchards spreading across the valleys. He spoke of mild winters and of the cooling mountain breezes that bathed the county in summer. Stanwell listened.

"And people," the client said. "There are hardly any."

Every house in Gilmer County outside of town came

with forty acres or more of privacy.

Stanwell listened hard and fast. A life in Gilmer County, Georgia, was just what he wanted. It was just what he needed. It was what he must have.

Stanwell had a new idea. He was going to spend the rest of his life writing novels. Literature was his first love. He'd never liked the law, not really. Law, as far as Stanwell was concerned, was the worst thing that had ever happened to language.

His client had just the place in mind, and Stanwell signed a mortgage without having yet seen his new home. He sold everything he owned except his typewriter and a few items of clothing. Stanwell bought a new car, a black Chevy two-door with a starter pedal on the floor. Into the trunk of the car, he packed reams of clean, white paper, four gross of yellow legal pads, a dozen boxes of pens and pencils, and enough spare typewriter ribbons to type *War and Peace* a thousand times. The rear of his car was so heavy that by the time he left the city, the headlights on the Chevy pointed slightly up from the road, toward heaven.

It was night and it was raining on Highway 74 in the mountains just north of Cherrylog, Georgia, when Chaucer introduced himself to his new owner.

A white-looking dog stood in the rain in the middle of the road. Stanwell, his heart racing, slowed down as best he could and swerved into the facing lane of wet blacktop. He made it safely around the dog in the road. Thankfully, no other cars were coming.

Stanwell slowed to a stop on the empty highway, his

brake lights shining bright red in the rain. The white dog watched him, waiting, but didn't budge an inch until Stanwell leaned across and popped open the passenger door. Chaucer trotted to the car and climbed inside, smelling strongly of wet dog.

The dog sat up in the seat on his front legs and stared out the windshield. Stanwell was forced to get out of his side of the Chevy and hurry around the front of the car to close the passenger door. By the time he was back in the driver's seat, he was nearly as wet as the dog.

The dog with one flop-tipped ear barked once, still staring out the windshield at the empty highway. The wipers swished back and forth like dog tails set to medium-fast wag. Stanwell put the Chevy in gear and got up speed.

The dog's coat was matted. His belly and feet were the color of mud. Stanwell thought of *The Canterbury Tales*, of wayfaring strangers climbing in and out of carriages, each one with a fascinating story to tell. He named the dog Chaucer on the spot.

"Where are you headed, friend?" Stanwell asked his new passenger.

But he already knew the answer. Chaucer was headed home. When the car door opened, it was the cover of a book. Chaucer jumped right inside the pages of Stanwell's life, where he would live until the last chapter.

Stanwell Perpett's house, located three-quarters of a mile up a rutted clay driveway from the main road, was nestled in rural tranquility. He and Chaucer liked living there. Chaucer, less than a year old the night they met, craved large doses of attention. Stanwell was happy to oblige. But he also had work to do. He cut a hole in the back door and hung it with a piece of heavy carpet so Chaucer could come and go as he pleased.

The ex-lawyer worked feverishly on his writing in an upstairs room that was actually the refurbished attic. It had a window at either end. He crafted stories of grand passions, of characters caught up in thrilling conflict and decisive action. He typed long into the night, often saying aloud the words of the sentences he so carefully crafted.

Chaucer, curled on the rug, listened to every word as the logs in the fireplace downstairs burned slowly into glowing coals and, finally, embers.

Stanwell drove the Chevy to a little grocery store three towns away for supplies. He didn't want to know his neighbors. It might keep him from working. He learned to live in the country and learned to like it. He forgot to buy a television set. Stanwell learned to chop firewood into kindling and to build a roaring blaze in the fireplace without using wadded-up newspaper. He fiddled with the pump on the well when it stopped working and got it going again. He planted roses and daffodil bulbs he ordered from a catalog.

Chaucer watched his master's activity with rapt attention, as if Stanwell were teaching the dog how to do human chores. Chaucer must have had trouble with some aspect of planting bulbs, because he dug them all up so he could watch Stanwell plant them again.

And Chaucer taught Stanwell a few things. He taught the middle-aged bachelor to come out on the porch after

the thunder was over and to listen to the sibilant sound of
rain on the pines. It sounded like people talking in hushed
voices. He taught Stanwell to throw a stick into the old
pond out back so Chaucer would have a reason to jump in.
He taught Stanwell, by insistent demonstration, that it was
never too cold to swim, and that any good dog knew how
to shake water from his fur in an arching spray, so that his
master would get wet, too, and not miss out on any of the
fun. Sometimes, Chaucer had to chase Stanwell down to do
it properly. It was hard to run with all that water in your
coat, but Chaucer didn't mind. He'd catch Stanwell over by
the tree or at the back door and listen to the human holler
when Chaucer finally shook the frigid pond water on him.
People made such funny noises. Chaucer wished he knew
what all that noise meant. It was too bad, really, that humans couldn't learn to bark.

Stanwell finished his first novel. It was terrific. He painstakingly typed sixteen copies of the manuscript and sent
them to his primary list of the publishers in New York.

It rained the day Stanwell received his first return. The
rejected manuscript got soaked, sticking halfway out of the
mailbox down by the main road. That didn't help any. He
didn't blame the letter carrier for refusing to make the trek
up his rutted clay road to deliver packages. But that was
only half the problem. Mailing the precious manuscripts
and keeping them dry would mean standing all morning in
the road with an umbrella. If the wind were blowing, even
an umbrella wouldn't do the trick.

Having become quite self-sufficient, Stanwell solved the

problem. He collected stones from his property. He dug them with a shovel like a kid digging worms for bait. Chaucer helped as best he could by digging his own holes all over the place. He didn't know what they were mining, but it definitely smelled good to open the earth. It was delicious. Once he had enough stones to work with, the novelist built a little rock house for his mailbox. It had a pointed roof and an arched opening. He made it big enough to set packages inside. Neighbors who drove by called it the Elf House. Stanwell Perpett's place has been known throughout southern Gilmer County by that name ever since.

Something was wrong with his first novel. It wasn't just right. As more and more publishing houses returned the manuscript, Stanwell found that he liked people less and less.

He would do better on the next one. He went to work right away. He typed all day and revised at night.

Chaucer would come into the room to listen for a while, then try to coax his master outside, where all the good things were. He'd sniff a little. Then he'd whimper. And when he was through whimpering, Chaucer did a few whines and concluded his lecture with a couple of sharp barks.

"What is it, fella?" Stanwell would say without looking up, his concentration broken. Then he'd turn to look at Chaucer and say, "What's up, doc?" It was one of the human's favorite phrases.

Stanwell patted his own leg. Chaucer danced to his master's side and let the writer pet his head a bit. The human seemed to like doing that. It kept him from being lonely.

"What do you think of this, Chaucer?" Stanwell read him a few lines. "Does it sound okay to you? Do you think that's the way I should say it?"

Chaucer gave up. He went downstairs and outside to the pond. He barked a little, but no one showed up to throw in a stick. So he walked around the pond and sniffed at all the damp places at the water's edge.

Chaucer's fat tail went to swinging. He found something he'd never seen before. He put his front paws out and lowered his white face for a closer look. He touched it with his nose. It didn't bite. It made the funniest little noise to boot. Chaucer couldn't believe his luck. His tail never stopped wagging.

Now, this was something he was sure his human would like. And there were more than one of them! Heck, who cared if the human liked them or not? Chaucer was bringing them home.

Upstairs, Stanwell paced the room with sheets of typing paper in his hands. He read passages aloud, emphasizing the poetry of each balanced sentence. His life's ambition was to be a published novelist, no matter what. He walked in circles as he read, chasing his dream around the room with relentless energy, trying to catch it in both hands.

Chaucer watched from the doorway. It was odd to watch the human walk in circles. If only the poor guy had a tail to chase. There wasn't anything Chaucer could do about that. Dogs were born with all the advantages. Humans had to learn to make do. They could carry almost nothing in their mouths. Humans had to give up two of their legs for carrying things around with. And because of this, they couldn't run half as well as they needed to. It was a wonder that there were any humans left at all, that bears and mountain lions hadn't come out of the woods, chased them down, and eaten every one of them. Chaucer would have to remember to bark a lot to give his human a head start if any of the really big animals came around the place.

But right now, he had something else on his mind. Something little. Something in his mouth.

"What the heck is that?" Stanwell said, getting up from his chair. "Chaucer!"

As the novelist approached, Chaucer turned away. The prize still cradled snugly in his gentle mouth, he walked purposefully out of the room, down the stairs, and into the kitchen. Stanwell followed.

Chaucer lowered his mouth and released a small ball of downy whitish yellow on the floor. It wobbled as if it wanted to roll, then stopped. It made a tiny sound like the start of a door coming open. Bending closer, Stanwell saw that it had two big feet and a head kept close to its body. It was a baby duck.

There were three more in the kitchen. Chaucer sat on his haunches and looked from one baby duck to another, to yet another, and then to the fourth. He was counting.

"Chaucer," Stanwell moaned, "what have you done? Where did these come from?"

Stanwell knew the answer.

He layered the bottom of a milk crate with torn strips of grocery sacks. Proudly, Chaucer nosed the last two along as the writer scooped up the baby ducks and placed them one by one inside the crate.

"They're going back, you know."

Stanwell bent over and took Chaucer's face in both hands, looking carefully at the edges of his mouth. He checked to see if Chaucer's nose had been bitten. Chaucer didn't mind. He thought the attention was a reward for having added such delightful little creatures to the household. Stanwell checked Chaucer's front paws. He was looking for signs of blood. There were none.

Stanwell picked up the crate and hurried outside. Carrying the crate well out in front of him so the squeaking little cargo wouldn't bounce, he marched rapidly along the faded ruts of an old tractor road, Chaucer at his side.

For Chaucer, it was like being in a parade. Dogs love a parade. They understand the point of it instantly. And no breed is born with a better talent for promenading than is the Golden Retriever. Whether from his mother or father, Chaucer had also inherited the gentle mouth of the breed. Few dogs can transport baby ducks over a distance of terrain without harming them. Golden Retrievers can, and so can half Golden Retrievers with one upright ear and one ear bent over at the tip.

Stanwell hurried to the edge of the pond. He set down the milk crate in the tall grass, found a long stick nearby, and began a methodical walk around the circumference of the pond. Chaucer put his white face inside the crate and counted ducks. The ducklings crowded to nuzzle his snout.

"Come on!" Stanwell yelled over his shoulder. "Show

me where you found them. Come on, boy!"

Chaucer loped to his master's side, looked around a minute, then hurried back to the crate of fuzzy ducklings. He pushed his face inside and counted. He touched each one with his nose. Dogs can count as high as six. Making sure four baby ducks were present and accounted for was easy math.

Stanwell circled the pond, probing the shadows at the water's edge with his stick. A frog jumped from its hidden spot into the water. Stanwell studied the water for a moment. Nothing was there but the usual bugs, algae, and duckweed. He searched carefully among a narrow stand of cattails in a shallow spot. He walked away from the pond a few feet and made a wider circle, kicking at clumps of weeds, poking his stick into thick mounds of bent-over blades of grass.

Chaucer joined him briefly, smelling the ground for nothing in particular, then hurried back to his arithmetic of ducks.

It was on Stanwell's third pass around the pond that he found it. There wasn't much left. The ground was torn in a small circle, where adult feathers were strewn. The mother duck had been killed, then torn apart and eaten. There were bits of blood, a few wing feathers, and nothing else.

It hadn't been Chaucer. Stanwell had already checked for signs of battle. There were none.

It was a coyote, Stanwell figured, or wild dogs. If the mother duck hadn't had offspring nearby, she would have flown away. Instead, she probably fled across the water to lead the hungry intruders away from her nest, then away from the pond altogether.

Later, Stanwell sat in a kitchen chair sipping coffee. He'd found an old bath towel and added it to the milk-crate habitat. He watched Chaucer lift the fuzzy ducklings from the crate one by one and place them on the floor. The dog pushed them with his nose, herding them into a group, then picked them up again one by one and carried them to his water bowl. He got all four to take a quick swim. He pushed them out when he thought they'd had enough.

Chaucer lay down on his side, his four legs sticking out, and rested his head on the floor. The ducklings came to him immediately. Chaucer managed to push them into a line along his belly. Stanwell watched in amazement as the ducklings backed against the soft fur of the dog's belly, shut their eyes, and went to sleep. Chaucer lay as still as if he were asleep, but his eyes were open, his eyebrows shifting now and then with his thoughts. He sighed.

Stanwell found out what baby ducks eat, then set about providing it. The four of them soon learned to quack and cluck their tongues. They followed Chaucer everywhere, gathering into a noisy ensemble at the bottom of the stairs whenever Chaucer, feeling the need to get away from his adopted ducklings, came up to visit Stanwell.

It wasn't long before the five made twice-daily trips to the pond. Chaucer picked up each one in his mouth and carried it out the dog door. Once they were outside, the four little ducks formed a waddling line behind Chaucer, who walked them to the water's edge. The ducks went into the water, swam, and found new things to eat, while Chaucer guarded the shore.

As summer ended, Stanwell finished his second novel. He typed multiple copies of the manuscript and sent it off. Fearful of rejection, he mailed two copies a day, so they wouldn't all come back at the same time. He walked them to the Elf House in the morning in their clean packaging, carefully weighed, the proper postage affixed, the addresses done neatly in indelible ink. He was followed by Chaucer and four ducks.

In the kitchen, each duck had its own towel. Chaucer moved the towels around at will. When he was done, the ducks found their appropriate places. The ducks ate dry dog food now, carrying morsels to the water bowl and dropping them in to soften them.

The ducks were noisier, too. They put up quite a racket when they felt like it. When Chaucer had enough of it, he barked sharply, and the ducks shut up.

Stanwell mopped the floor at least three times a day.

He set to work on his third book. The ideas for it had come in a flood of inspiration while he was still working on the second one.

As the manuscripts of the second novel began to be rejected and returned, Stanwell lost interest in getting the mail. Sometimes, he walked down to the little rock house no more than once a week.

The novelist kept Chaucer busy at night. He read lines to him over and over again. He explained the characters to Chaucer, and the dog always listened patiently. Stanwell needed someone to listen. He was losing his confidence.

"Nothing's up, doc," Stanwell would complain to his dog.

He snatched a page of manuscript and read it out loud.

"What do think of this? What would you say, Chaucer, if you were on vacation on the French Riviera and you came into your room to find your wife had been murdered on the bed? What if there was a dead man in the shower? What would you tell the cops? If her diamonds were missing, where would you look?"

Chaucer thought he might go back to the kitchen and count the ducks.

Winter came, and Stanwell found he had only a hundred pages done. He lost momentum. Grand passion was hard to come by.

The nights turned cold. Stanwell spent the mornings chopping firewood into kindling. Chaucer watched four adult ducks swim in circles in the pond. He would have jumped in with them, but it was his job to guard the shore. He understood that much.

It was when Stanwell set down his ax and picked up the hatchet to cut kindling sticks into long, narrow splinters that he realized what was happening. He set away his tools and walked to the pond.

"What's up, doc?" he said when Chaucer turned his head to watch his master approach.

Chaucer's tail thumped the ground. He could use some company. It took a lot of sitting to get ducks to grow.

Stanwell knelt beside his dog and put his arm over

Chaucer's shoulders. Chaucer licked Stanwell's cheek once to say hello. They watched the ducks swim close to shore. The ducks wanted to see what was going on.

"They should have left by now," Stanwell said. "It's going to be a record cold this winter."

Ducks are supposed to leave for cold winters. But Chaucer's ducks were too fat to flee the Appalachian foothills. Stanwell wasn't sure they even knew how to fly. They walked everywhere they went because Chaucer did. They were little dogs in their own minds, chubby little dogs with waterproof feathers and bills.

It happened in the morning. It had stayed well below freezing for three days, and the pond had frozen over during the night. Chaucer didn't mind the weather. He had a thick coat. Neither did his ducks mind the cold. You could see little clouds of vapor come from the ducks' bills as they walked in line along the tractor road to the frozen pond. It was the first time on ice for all four of them. They scooted madly upon the pond, falling to their bellies and sliding farther and farther as they kicked with their webbed feet to try to stand up.

A pack of wild dogs waited. Mixed-breed strays that had formed a family circle to survive, the dogs obeyed no rule of man and ate whatever they could find. Their nature was a vicious one, as alien to Chaucer as if they were tigers from a foreign jungle. The pack divided itself into a group of two and a group of three. One large black dog waited. The others circled the pond along either side.

Chaucer scented the intruders. It was an overpowering

smell of violence and danger. The fur lifted along his spine. He arched his back and bared his teeth, looking left and looking right, his head lowered.

The ducks were soon cut off. The dogs came onto the ice from either side while the black dog watched. Chaucer was outside the circle the dogs had formed around their prey, a circle that closed with every breath of crisp, winter air. Chaucer leapt onto the ice and pushed himself forward. Two of his ducks were dead by the time he reached the first dog.

The black dog at the end of the pond came fully alert. It barked a command. Two of the dogs turned to meet Chaucer. Chaucer slid into them with his teeth bared.

The noise of battle was immense. An unrestrained, shrill howl of pain brought Stanwell out the back door in his bare feet and underwear.

There was no mistaking the sound. It was Chaucer.

Stanwell ran across the frozen yard to the woodpile, where he picked up his ax without pausing. He ran hard all the way to the pond, ready to kill a bear if he had to.

"Stop it!" he yelled as he ran. "Stop it!"

By the time he got there, the wild dogs had carried away the bodies of the ducks. They were gone except for a few feathers stuck in frozen spots of blood on the ice. Stanwell could only guess how many dogs there had been.

Chaucer whimpered in grief and pain. He struggled to pull himself up from the growing pool of his own blood. His white coat was stained red in several places. He'd been savagely bitten, his flesh torn and holed. Blood poured from his mouth. But his bones still worked, and he did his best to stand up, which he accomplished. His body trembled when he tried to take a step. His legs shook, and he found he couldn't walk. He stood on the ice, his head down, and shivered.

Stanwell Perpett ran onto the ice as if it were pavement. It cracked under his steps. Still he ran forward, dropping the ax, reaching Chaucer just as the dog collapsed from his wounds. He scooped the bloodied dog into his arms. The ice gave way under them, and Stanwell found himself standing barelegged in hip-deep ice water. He didn't stop to breathe. He turned toward home, his dog clutched high to his chest, and marched through the breaking ice until he reached the pond's edge.

He wept as he ran, gasping for air, his legs burning, his vision blurred. Barging into the house, he wrapped Chaucer in a blanket and hurriedly put on some clothes. He didn't bother drying his feet or legs. He didn't tie his shoes or lock the door behind him when he left. Stanwell carried his mangled companion to the Chevy and arranged him in the backseat. Chaucer was breathing, but he was not awake. The worst wound was along the side of his neck. Blood ran from his mouth, his neck.

The novelist had never in his life heard a more awful sound than Chaucer's mournful cry when the dogs bit into him. It had been a scream, really. Stanwell would never forget the sound of it.

He raced the car down the old, rutted driveway to the main road.

Chaucer's wounds were egregious ones. The end of his tongue had been bitten away, the remainder split to the middle of his mouth. Chaucer's throat was lacerated. There were deep wounds to his neck and shoulders, and the flesh of one hip had been torn away. The top of his face just behind his black nose had been punctured by a tooth. The wild dogs had gripped him from either end in their attack.

Stanwell visited him twice a day, every day, but it wasn't until the third day that Chaucer noticed him. He was wrapped in bandages front and rear, with tubes inserted to drain the wounds. The white dog thumped his tail when Stanwell stuck his fingers into the wire cage of Chaucer's recovery room.

"What's up, doc?" Stanwell said.

Chaucer thumped his tail again.

"It's a miracle he's alive," the vet said. "I've seen dogs hit by trucks that didn't come in as bad as this."

Chaucer was indeed alive. Ten days later, he was home and on the mend. Chaucer didn't look for the ducks. He knew they were dead. Stanwell could tell that Chaucer missed them. And so did he, a little bit.

One black lip sagged from having been torn and re-paired with stitches. And Chaucer had a little trouble drink-ing with his shortened, split tongue. But more importantly, his throat was healing. He was able to swallow.

Something, though, had damaged his vocal cords. The sounds he made sounded to Stanwell like human sounds. Chaucer developed the habit of clearing his throat. You'd

264   *Elf House*

have sworn that a full-grown man was in the doorway trying to get your attention. When Chaucer barked, it sounded something like a cough.

Chaucer gave voice to his feelings. When he was tired, he sighed in such a way that Stanwell looked up from his work to see what lovely woman had come into his room. When Chaucer was happy, he laughed. It was a little like someone panting with joy, a little like human laughter deep in the throat.

Stanwell believed his dog was learning to talk.

Chaucer learned something else. He learned to be intolerant of visitors, be they dog or man. He would scramble down the rutted clay drive in a mad tear, barking at the letter carrier's car when it paused in front of the Elf House to pick up or deliver mail.

The mailman said it sounded like someone was shouting at him, Chaucer's bark was so altered.

"It was just like someone hollering for you to get the heck out of there," he said. "And here would come that dog at full run right at the car. Well, I never lingered much after that. The Elf House was never my favorite stop."

Chaucer practiced with his repaired throat and shortened tongue. He created entirely new sounds in his attempt to make the dogs sounds he had always lived by.

When the writer pulled himself from his desk chair to come downstairs to feed Chaucer in the kitchen, he always asked, "Hungry, boy? Are you hungry, boy?"

Of course he was hungry. It had been all day since he'd eaten anything more than a stick he'd found in the backyard. Chaucer lifted the guttural purr that is common to Golden Retrievers from the back of his damaged throat toward the front of his mouth. Coming down the stairs in front of Stanwell, who was always too slow when it came to food, Chaucer went about his hungry noises, his wind punctuated by landing his weight on a wooden step below. The minor jolt interrupted his eager, time-to-eat, deep-voiced whine, and he spoke for the first time.

"Hungry boy," Chaucer said. Or something very much like it.

The novelist froze in midstep. Chaucer stopped at the bottom of the stairs to look over his shoulder at his master, intolerant of any delay.

"What?" Stanwell asked. "What did you say?"

"Hungry," Chaucer said.

He padded on into the kitchen.

"Hungry hungry hungry," he said, a bit curious about his own accomplishment.

He seemed to know what he was saying and delighted in the new sound and the way it felt coming over his throat.

"Hungry hungry hungry hungry."

"Okay, I get it!" Stanwell said.

He lifted the food bowl to the countertop and opened the cupboard to measure a cup and a half of dry dog food.

"Hungry hungry hungry hungry." Chaucer added a little woof at the end, and it came out "Hungry boy."

Stanwell shook his head. He grinned. It was too much. He laughed. He had a talking dog on his hands.

"Hungry hungry hungry boy."

Chaucer went on and on. He shut up when the food bowl was on the floor, and not a second sooner.

When Chaucer was through eating, he buried his muzzle in the water. Stanwell had placed it on the seat of a kitchen chair because the dog had so much trouble drinking once his tongue had healed. Chaucer would fill his mouth with water and lift his black nose high, as if he were pointing to the moon. He would gulp at the water as it came into the back of his mouth and down his throat. He learned to swallow like a human.

When he was through, he shook his head from side to side to fling off the tickle of water on his chin. His tongue went to the top of his mouth, and he whistled. The sound so startled him that he did it again.

Chaucer went around whistling for days. He went outside and whistled at the birds and squirrels. He whistled at the trees. He came upstairs, pausing at each step to whistle, then whistled going back downstairs.

"You have to stop that," Stanwell scolded him. "People whistle for dogs to come, not the other way around."

"Hungry hungry hungry," Chaucer muttered. "Hungry hungry hungry boy."

Chaucer liked being able to talk. He was getting more food, sometimes as much as three bowlfuls a day. And there were plenty of snacks. Stanwell laid in a large supply of dog biscuits and would toss him one whenever he needed the dog to shut up.

Chaucer learned to say *no*. It had been Stanwell's favorite word when they first moved into the house. Chaucer never liked hearing it, but he got a real kick out of saying it.

"Hungry hungry hungry," Chaucer said.

"Go away. I'm working."

Stanwell had work to do. His fourth novel was taking shape on the page. It was a doozie.

"No."

"Go now, I said!"

"No." Saying *no* was as easy as woofing. Nothing to it. "No no no. No no no. No!"

Eventually, Chaucer would give up. He'd tramp downstairs and whistle until Stanwell showed up and got a dog biscuit out of the cupboard.

The novelist was at his wit's end. He couldn't get in an hour's work without interruption. He put both hands on the kitchen counter, leaned his head forward, closed his eyes, and thought hard. Something had to be done about this.

"What's up, doc?" Chaucer asked. It was the first time he'd put three words together. Of course, he knew them by heart.

"I'm buying earplugs," Stanwell replied, as if he'd been asked by a person what was on his mind. "The kind swimmers use. Then I'm getting a pair of earmuffs."

"Hungry hungry hungry," Chaucer said.

Stanwell felt like crying. He loved Chaucer, but he couldn't take the dog's relentless request for food any longer.

"All right, then," the novelist said. "If you're going to talk, then you're going to learn to talk! A little variety of expression is called for. And you must stop whistling, do you hear me? No more whistling!"

"Hungry hungry hungry," Chaucer repeated. He enjoyed talking better than he liked to listen.

Stanwell bought a book on teaching parrots to speak. He learned that birds with split tongues develop fabulous vocabularies. If birds could do it, he reasoned, so could Chaucer.

The dog's lessons began in earnest. Stanwell drew pictures in an effort to teach Chaucer a few simple nouns. Verbs were a little more difficult, but Chaucer picked up quickly on the ones that involved him. He learned to say "Pat my head" and "Pick me up."

Between lessons, Stanwell finished his fourth novel and his fifth. He spent a small fortune on postage.

Chaucer grew old. The white dog with one flop-tipped ear finally quit whistling.

Book six was a real bugger.

"Chaucer! Come here!"

Chaucer climbed the stairs, more slowly than in years past.

"What's up?" he said. "What's up, doc?"

"Listen to this, will you?"

Stanwell read him a few pages of dialogue.

Chaucer wasn't interested. He lay down on the rug and put his head on his front legs, one side of his lip curled up. He could snore with the best of them, and that's what he had in mind to do.

"Well, what do you think?" Stanwell asked when he was through reading.

Chaucer opened his eyes.

"Bad," he said. "Bad ugly." He closed his eyes again. "Bad bad bad."

"What's bad, Chaucer? It's not bad, not really. Is it?"

"No ducks," Chaucer said, keeping his eyes closed.

As he fell asleep, sometimes he remembered the ducks.

<hr />

People in Gilmer County remember Stanwell Perpett as a hermit. They say he lived alone in the Elf House, a two-story clapboard nestled deep in the woods.

It wasn't true. He had Chaucer.

There's a dog's grave in the overgrown backyard of the abandoned house. Stanwell is buried in a cemetery nearby. None of his writing ever saw publication. Yet.

Stanwell may still be writing. The locals say that on certain nights, a light can be seen in the upstairs window of the dilapidated house. If you get close enough, you can hear the rhythmic *tip-tap* of someone typing. If you get really close and are quiet, late at night, you can hear Stanwell talking to himself, reading lines from his work-in-progress.

According to legend, the house is haunted. And so is the yard.

Kids from the high school sometimes drive out to the Elf House to test the legend. A sophomore, Steven Bale, known by the nickname "Skeeter," had something to prove to the older boys. He was skinny and couldn't fight well, but that didn't mean he lacked courage. After school, he told everyone that he was going to the Elf House that night, that he would walk right up to the empty house at midnight, knock on the door, and wait to see what happened.

Two of the older boys, David Patton and Jack Mills, both juniors, agreed to go along. They'd report back truthfully what happened. If Skeeter chickened out, it would be all over school. If he didn't, he'd have a brand-new reputation as someone who wasn't afraid of anything—not even ghosts.

They met at the end of town in the Dairy Queen parking lot. The two older boys rode in their own car, following Skeeter. He drove the winding country roads until he came to the little stone mail house. Skeeter found a place to park. The older boys parked right behind him. At ten minutes to midnight, they got out of their cars. The older boys would come along to see what happened. They planned to lag behind a bit.

It was a particularly dark night. The old rutted lane leading up to the house was overgrown in low briars. The road was pitted in several places, as if someone had been digging holes. Large rocks littered the path. The boulders looked as if they'd tumbled from higher ground, where the dirt had washed out in a heavy rain. Perhaps someone had pushed them there.

They started up the road, Skeeter going first. The three boys had flashlights, which helped a little. Still, the going was rough. Cockleburs soon clung to their pant legs and socks. The flashlight beams created the sensation that there were moving shadows to their left and right. One of the older boys directed his light high into the branches of a tree, where he thought there might be bats. He didn't see any.

When they reached the house, there was no light on in the upstairs window. No one could be heard typing inside.

Skeeter stood at the outer edge of the rotted porch boards. He wondered whether the old wood would hold his weight. Ready to step up to the task at hand, he put his flashlight beam on the front door. It was splintered and cracked. The knob had been broken off. The black inner darkness of the house peeked out at him.

He shone his light on a near window, one overlooking the porch. The glass had been broken out long ago. The whole place was falling down. He put one foot on the porch. The boards creaked.

Then he heard a dog bark. It sounded as if it came from around the back of the house. It wasn't a friendly bark. The barking circled the house, coming to the front. It was a big dog, you could tell. And now, just now, he heard a vicious, low growling of a dog about to attack, a dog that sure as shooting was one that would bite.

"Dog!" one of the other boys shouted.

The two turned to run back to their car.

"It's here!" Skeeter screamed.

He could hear it breathing. The dog was upon him. He didn't have time to shine his flashlight in a circle to see the dog. Instead, he ran a few steps toward the trees. The dog was right behind him. Skeeter didn't know why he wasn't already bitten. He flung himself toward a tree, stuffing the flashlight in his belt. With a lunge, he began climbing.

Someone whistled.

Skeeter pulled himself onto the lowest branch, stood

on it to reach the one above, and kept climbing. He'd seen vicious dogs leap halfway up a tree trunk. And this dog sounded as mean as they came. It circled the tree, snarling, stamping the weeds and overgrown grass into a path.

From his lofty perch, Skeeter saw the lights of the car parked behind his vehicle come to life. He listened to the car pull away, watched its taillights disappear over a hill.

He was alone.

The dog growled and occasionally barked, still circling the tree. Skeeter retrieved his flashlight and directed the beam toward the ground, expecting to see a bloodthirsty hound snarling up at him.

He didn't see a thing. There was no dog. Yet he'd been treed by the sound of a dog. It was a ghost dog, he was sure. No one had said anything about a dog. Skeeter wasn't coming down. The growling was real.

The sounds subsided after a long while. Skeeter saw a car approach on the road below the house. He flashed his light in that direction, signaling. The driver didn't see it and continued on by.

The dog or ghost, whatever it was, had tramped back toward the house, but Skeeter could hear it breathing not far away. Not far enough.

He didn't like being in the tree, but he was afraid to come down. When he thought he couldn't hear the dog breathing, he shook one of the smaller branches near him to see what would happen. The barking started instantly, the growling, the sound of a dog rushing from the deeper darkness to the bottom of the tree.

Skeeter tried his flashlight again. There was nothing there. Nothing you could see. He turned the flashlight off to save the batteries in case another car came by. Someone whistled. Maybe the owner was coming to get the dog. The dog's breathing was louder than before. It remained close by.

No, he thought, *nobody comes to get a ghost dog*.

He adjusted his position, trying to get comfortable, trying to find a place where he could relax. Trees are not very comfortable, especially at night. Then Skeeter thought about ants. Ants live in trees. Soon, they would be crawling on him. He had to move away from the leaves.

Being in a tree at night, all alone like that, the minutes seemed like an eternity. He thought he might be there for the rest of his life.

Skeeter leaned to his left, and the flashlight fell. It came on when it hit the ground. The ghost dog barked, growled, came forward, and picked the flashlight up in its mouth. It circled the tree. Skeeter wanted to scream. The light, held a foot or two off the ground, circled the tree. He thought he heard someone mumbling.

The flashlight came to rest in the yard halfway between the tree and the house.

Skeeter stared at the distant circle of light, watching it grow dim. Then the dog was back. It growled. It pawed the ground. It whined in frustration. Skeeter thought he heard its claws scratch at the tree trunk. Then it stopped moving. He could hear it panting. This time, it was going to leave.

"What's up, doc?" someone said from the ground, startling Skeeter.

No one was there.

"Bad ugly," the deep-throated voice said.

"Hello?" Skeeter spoke softly. "Hello?" His voice trembled. He listened closely.

The dog was walking again, circling.

"Hungry hungry hungry," the voice said. "Hungry boy."

An hour later, David Patton and Jack Mills arrived with reinforcements. Two carloads of boys climbed the rutted path. They carried sticks. One had a lantern.

Skeeter watched their approach.

"Over here," he said. "I'm in the tree."

"Come on down," David said. "The dog's gone."

"Yeah, I know."

"Well, come on down then. We're sorry we left you so long. Was it bad up there?"

Skeeter scrambled to the lower branch. His shoes were bathed in the upper circle of the lantern's glow. He jumped to the ground, falling forward on his hands when he hit. He got up quickly.

"It wasn't too bad," he said. "Someone came by I could talk to."

Skeeter never told anyone that the dog was a ghost, and that ghost dogs in Georgia know how to talk. He'd drive by the Elf House now and again and leave an open box of dog biscuits in the arch-roofed rock structure where the mailbox had once been. Sometimes, he heard a whistle before he left.

Belly Dog

Fearn Corners, Mississippi

During the early years of our Great Depression, the bluebirds left Noxubee County, Mississippi. Poor John was among the first to notice they were gone.

"They left for lack of rain," he told his wife.

The ground in Noxubee County was as dry as toast. The corn Poor John planted dried on the stalk without coming to tassel. The tomato plants failed to flower at all. There wasn't one tomato in the yard. The plants looked like dried-up old men with skeleton arms. Times were tough because of the drought. The rooster didn't get up in the morning, and the chickens quit laying eggs.

Poor John washed turnips early one morning in a big galvanized washtub that had only one hole in it. He hadn't slept well the night before. The sound of growling stomachs in his little shack had kept him awake. That pitiful rumbling would have kept him awake till the rooster crowed, if they hadn't already eaten him.

He didn't sleep well, when he could sleep at all, knowing there wouldn't be any bluebirds in the yard in the morning. There wouldn't be any bluebirds in the trees along the road either. There wasn't a bluebird to be seen in all of Noxubee County, and that was a shame. It meant that things would get worse before they got any better.

The well was low. He used as little water as possible to wash the turnips. Poor John needed to get the turnips clean. It was important to have clean turnips when it came time to trade. Some of the men thereabouts didn't understand that, but Poor John did. Times like these, dirty turnips were worth almost nothing at all. Clean ones weren't worth much more.

He was taking a whole sack of them to the little grocery store at Fearn Corners, where the two roads crossed to the west of Mashulaville, to see what he could trade them for. Bacon, he hoped, and maybe some eggs. A small sack of cornmeal would come in handy.

He had plenty of turnips. And there were dried beans

in the cellar. The family would be eating beans and turnip soup until the pecan crop came in. You needed pork bones to put in beans and in turnip soup, either one. Maybe he'd get some pork bones, too.

The pecans this year would be everything to Poor John and his family. There wouldn't be many because of the drought. But there would be some. Of course, the pecans wouldn't fall till autumn, and it was only summer now. To-morrow, if he were lucky, he'd catch a fish or two from his creek. It wasn't running anymore. But there were still some deep, muddy puddles, and Poor John thought there might be a fish or two left. Might not.

"Old lady," he said to his wife, "it's a long walk, and I best be going now. Tell the boys when they get around to throw rocks at the squirrels when they see them. They just might get one today. I feel like they might."

"John, you're always feeling things."

"Yes, ma'am," he said. John felt a change coming. It was just a small tickle of a feeling.

"Sometimes they happen," his wife said. "And some-times they don't."

That was the funny thing about feelings, Poor John figured.

It was still early in the morning, but it was already hot. There wasn't a cloud in the sky to shade Mississippi from the summer sun. The dirt road was deep with dust. Poor John hefted his gunnysack of clean turnips to one shoulder and began his long walk. He wouldn't walk this way at night, no sir. The road to Fearn Corners led by the old Perchman plantation, where Poor John's grandfather had been born a slave. The farm had been cut into smaller pieces and sold off long ago, but the hanging tree was still there, right by the road. And so was the Perchman family cemetery, where the one-legged graverobber had been caught by a ghost back in his grandfather's day.

His mother had told the story when Poor John was a little boy.

There was a big, flat rock between the cemetery and the road. It had a line of holes in it, like deep footprints. Some people said the holes were drilled by Choctaw Indians hundreds of years ago for purposes no one now could figure. Poor John knew how the holes got there. His mother had told him.

"My pappy was a freedman then," she said. "Like the others, though, he still worked the plantation and got nothing for it but old."

When Mistress Perchman died, they buried her with a gold watch pinned to her clothes. Poor John's grandfather and two other freedmen dug the grave. They covered it up when the funeral was over. One of them told all the others about the gold watch.

"They put some money in there with her, too," he said, "to pay her fare across the river."

The river was the River Jordan. All the dead had to cross that river to get into heaven.

"You don't need a gold watch in heaven," the one-legged freedman said.

Nobody remembered his name, according to Poor John's

mother. Poor John thought maybe she did know. But you don't tell name stories on the dead. Not in Mississippi, anyway. They'll come back to get you if you do.

The one-legged freedman talked a friend into pushing him in a wheelbarrow to the plantation cemetery that night. They took a shovel along. When they got there, it was very dark. They couldn't light a lantern, or someone might see them. The two-legged man dug in the dark. A one-legged man isn't much good with a shovel.

The two-legged man got down to the coffin soon enough. The one-legged man, sitting in his wheelbarrow, leaned far over to look inside the grave. It was too dark to see anything in the hole.

"Get the lid off of her," he urged the other man. "Get the shovel under the edge and pry it off."

It was awkward work, but he managed it. The nails pulling out of the wood made an awful screech.

"Now feel around and find that watch."

"I don't like touching a dead person," the digger complained.

"You want the watch or don't you?"

There isn't much room to stand in a grave. The two-legged man leaned way over with his hands outstretched. He leaned down low. Just as he was about to touch the buried woman's clothes, his feet slipped, and he fell forward with a yell. He fell right on top of the dead woman. Her cold, dead face was against his.

You fall on a dead person, the first thing you want to do is get right off. The only way out of a grave is straight up. There's no debate. And that's what that fellow did. He jumped straight up with his whole body. Being scared out of his mind, he jumped up from lying flat, all six feet in one big push, until, just like that, he was standing on the ground at the edge of the grave.

The one-legged man took to hollering something fierce.

The dead woman had stuck to the gravedigger somehow. Maybe it was the watch. Or maybe her clothes were sticky from being buried in a pine box. Either way, she stuck to him head to foot, like they were dancing close. She wouldn't let go of him.

What the one-legged man saw was the woman standing atop her own grave. It was light enough to see that much.

He didn't wait for her to say a thing. He took to hollering and jumped out of his wheelbarrow and ran all the way back to his home, which was two miles the other side of the creek.

One-legged men don't run unless they have to. This one pumped his arms high in the air and hit the ground moving as fast as a train on a downhill track. Most folks when they run throw one foot in front of the other. The one-legged man ran by waving his arms for balance and tossing that one foot in front of one foot, then out in front of the one foot again. At each bound, he left a deep hole in the dirt, packing it down so hard it turned to rock.

That rock's still there. So is the hanging tree.

Poor John shifted his sack of washed turnips to his other shoulder and trod on. His shoes and his pant legs were coated with dust. He crossed to the other side of the road, where he could find more shade.

On the other side of Fearn Corners, coming this way, a

stray dog trotted along the dirt road like he knew where he was going. He walked from town to town looking for handouts. But not the kind of handouts you think. He wanted his belly rubbed. He wanted a hand held out to pet him.

The little mutt usually walked along the railroad tracks. He'd find people there. He'd say hello when people acted like they wanted him to. He'd eagerly accept a hand to rub his belly. Then he'd be off again.

The little dog showed up in counties all over the South.

He had a spiky coat of gray hair, with black and some white, blended all together. And maybe there was a spot or two of brown. No one who met him could tell you for sure what color the dog was. His eyes were dark, most said. He had big eyes for a dog that size. His tail was short and straight. Others said it was long and curled up over his back. The tip of his tail was pure white, except for those who remembered that it was actually black.

Poor John hadn't eaten breakfast. Thinking about the grocery store at the crossroads sharpened his appetite. The sack of turnips grew heavier with every step. He set the sack down and mopped sweat from his forehead. They'd give him water at the store. They always did. Mr. Fearn's daughter, Amelia, gave him a glass to drink from. She was nice to everybody.

He reached the store at the same time the dog did. It hopped upon the porch from one side as Poor John set down his sack of turnips at the other end. He hoped they hadn't picked up too much dust on the long walk to Fearn Corners.

The spiky-haired dog met him in the middle. He trotted over to meet Poor John. When he got there, he rolled over on his back.

Poor John looked down and smiled. He bent way over and gave the dog a rub on his belly.

"Where you from, little fella? I haven't seen you here before."

One of the hard-luck farmers from the area swung open the screen door from the inside, and Poor John straightened up.

"Mornin'," Poor John said. "This your dog?"

"Wouldn't have a dog that small," the farmer said.

The screen door banged behind him. He was carrying a gunnysack that looked much like Poor John's. The farmer, pressed by the difficulties of his own poverty, found his manners.

"How are you?" he asked Poor John.

"Fine, just fine," Poor John said. "Sure do wish it would rain, though."

"Don't hold your breath," the farmer said.

He stepped over the upturned little dog and walked away.

"He probably didn't wash his turnips," Poor John said to the dog, rubbing his pink belly one or two more times.

Then he picked up his sack of produce and went inside. The little dog rolled up onto his four feet and walked to the edge of the porch. He looked up at the sky for a minute, then came back into the shade. He found a place to sit under a crude pine bench against the wall.

Amelia wasn't there today. Instead, her father stood

behind the counter, shaking his head at Poor John. They talked briefly. The grocer wanted something paid on Poor John's bill.

"I have no money today," Poor John said. "But I brought these fine turnips to trade. They're fat ones, they are, and as clean as a train whistle. They're fine turnips indeed, Mr. Fearn."

"Don't need no turnips, John. Everybody has turnips. I can't sell them. And if I can't sell them, I can't be taking them in on trade."

"You haven't seen these turnips, Mr. Fearn. They're very fine turnips, the best kind."

Outside, clouds took over the clear sky. If the men had been listening, they would have heard the first, light sounds of thunder.

Poor John set down the sack of turnips. He wanted to ask for a drink of water but decided to wait. He needn't be using up his favors.

"Maybe I could pick up a little something for the children on credit," Poor John said. "Half a dozen eggs and a bit of bacon."

"No more credit," Mr. Fearn said plainly, looking away from his customer.

"I'll have some money come pecan season, Mr. Fearn. Always do."

Poor John looked around at the advertising signs. He couldn't read letters, but he was good with numbers. One sign was a picture of a bottle of soda pop. The sign on the cigar box said two for five cents.

"No more credit, John. I'm truly sorry, but I can't pay

the lights the way it is. Besides, there won't be any pecans if we don't get some rain."

Poor John looked down at his dusty shoes. It felt bad, a full-grown man like him wanting to cry. He didn't know what to do.

"I sure wish I could trade these turnips," he said softly, as much to himself as to Mr. Fearn.

Mr. Fearn glanced out the window. It was suddenly dark outside.

"All right then," he said. "Let me take a look at what you got there."

Poor John reached into the gunnysack and pulled out a turnip in each hand. They were the best of the bunch. He handed them across the counter to Mr. Fearn.

"Holy cow, John. I swear, these are the finest turnips I've ever seen. Are the rest of them just like these?"

"Yes, sir," Poor John said, smiling. Fat raindrops fell against the window. "Twenty-five pounds of perfect turnips."

"I'll take them," Mr. Fearn said quickly. "You find what you need, and we'll tally up. Don't you rob me blind, you hear? Just what you need."

While Mr. Fearn removed the turnips from their sack, admiring each one as if it were a work of art, Poor John picked up a dozen eggs and a corner of bacon from the cooler in back. He found a small sack of cornmeal. And butter, just a stick. And a little flour for biscuits.

"Listen to that, will you?" Mr. Fearn said, placing the items Poor John had brought to the counter into his customer's gunnysack.

"Yes, sir, it's raining."

"It's not just raining, John. It's raining cats and dogs." Mr. Fearn smiled.

It was the first time Poor John had seen the old man do that.

"Like cats and dogs fighting, my momma always said."

"Like cats and dogs fighting, then," Mr. Fearn said. He laughed a little.

Poor John grinned.

"What you got there, John, is two dollars against your bill, and eighty-five cents hard money. How does that sound to you?"

"Sounds like I should buy a chicken," Poor John said. He felt like dancing. You can't underestimate the importance of washing your turnips when it comes time to trade. "Pick me out a big one."

Mr. Fearn wrapped a chicken in white paper and put it in Poor John's gunnysack with the other things. He placed two silver quarters on the counter, and Poor John put one in each shoe. There were holes in his pants pockets.

On the porch, he watched the rain turn the dirt road to mud. It smelled wonderful, the rain. The bluebirds would come back to Noxubee County, he was sure. There'd be bushels of pecans.

He set his sack on the bench, and the little dog came out and rolled over on his back. Poor John reached into his gunnysack and shifted things around. He put the flour and cornmeal in the middle, where they wouldn't get wet. He put the eggs on top. Then he held one out in his hand.

"How about lunch, little fella?"

He patted the dog's belly, then broke the egg on the porch floor and watched the dog lap it up.

Poor John picked up his sack. It wasn't heavy at all. He should have worn a hat, but he didn't mind, really. He'd get wet on the long walk home, and so would the chicken. Wouldn't hurt it any. Wouldn't hurt it a bit.

The little dog was through eating and had rolled over on his back again. Poor John bent down with his sack over one shoulder and rubbed the dog's belly one last time.

"I wish things would go this well all the time," he said.

Then he stepped off the porch into the rain.

Poor John threw back his head and opened his mouth wide as he walked away from the store. He drank his fill of rain.

He kind of hoped the little dog might follow him home and stay for a spell. The dog could help chase the squirrels from the pecan grove. But Poor John knew it wouldn't happen. No dog worth its salt will walk by a hanging tree. They go the other way every time.

The spiky-haired dog had other places to go. Each human who rubbed his belly got three wishes granted, no more than that. Few chose their wishes as well as Poor John.

The stray jumped off the porch and trotted along the crossroads in a new direction. There were small splashes of rain from his every step. He skipped with his back legs once or twice, then trotted on.